Season of Light and Hope

For Douglas and Carrie,
John and Kellynn

"How can we thank God enough for you
in return for all the joy
we feel before our God because of you?"
(1 Thessalonians 3:9)
Christmas 2004

Season of Light and Hope

PRAYERS AND LITURGIES FOR ADVENT AND CHRISTMAS

Blair Gilmer Meeks

ABINGDON PRESS / Nashville

SEASON OF LIGHT AND HOPE
PRAYERS AND LITURGIES FOR ADVENT AND CHRISTMAS

This book is printed on acid-free paper.

Library of Congress Cataloging in Publication Data

Meeks, Blair Gilmer.
   Season of light and hope : prayers and liturgies for Advent and Christmas / Blair Gilmer
Meeks.
      p. cm.
   Includes index.
   ISBN 0-687-34234-1 (pbk. : alk. paper)
   1. Christmas service. 2. Advent services. I. Title.

BV199.C45M44 2005
264--dc22   2005001279

05 06 07 08 09 10 11 12 13 14 – 10 9 8 7 6 5 4 3 2 1

MANUFACTURED IN THE UNITED STATES OF AMERICA

Contents

Introduction

"Tomorrow Shall Be My Dancing Day"

We have an invitation to dance through Advent and Christmas, and we will dance all at once in the past, present, and future. We will become participants in an intricate reel with an uninterrupted company of dancers. We move in and out among the dancers and spin through time. We dance the joy of a long-ago birth, the gladness of Jesus' presence with us now, and the hope of his coming reign of peace. We dance till we learn to sing with assurance that Christ has come, Christ is with us, and Christ will come again. For this reason Advent and Christmas form one joyful season that celebrates the light overcoming the shadows and hope overtaking despair. We join the dance to celebrate God's Word made flesh in the person of Jesus Christ, the light of the world, who came to earth and pitched a tent to live among us. We already have the full story of Jesus' coming and the promise of his future, and we are hopeful, thankful people.

The question for worship planners is how to tell the story of Jesus' coming to those who are reluctant to join the dance. Some reluctance comes from satiation, from too much familiarity with the basics of a story too often told without imagination. Some comes from the strangeness of the story and the unwillingness of modern listeners to enter into the poetry. And there will be some persons in our congregations who do not really know the story at all; though they may have heard about the baby in the manger, many do not know what leads to this miraculous birth or why it shapes our lives today.

As storytellers—and that includes musicians, preachers, readers, leaders of prayer, dramatists, teachers, and dancers—we will try to engage all the senses and help listeners find their way toward an imaginative participation in this story. The telling will, in other words, lift up the images that lead us to see this as a story for today because it holds the truth about our future. Such a telling begins with a thorough reading of the biblical prophecies and birth accounts, and an understanding of their significance for the story of God's love for us in the gift of God's Son, our crucified and risen Savior.

The story the Scriptures tell at Christmas begins with the plight of the poor and the outcast. That is the risk we take: to tell a story about the birth of a poor baby for whom there was no room in Rome's imperial scheme of things, and yet a story of such incredible joy and hope that we sing it, time and time again, using the most glorious hymns we can find.

The Christmas story is a foreshadowing of the whole story. Jesus comes in a time of great trouble and strife. There is constant terror from the Roman soldiers whose actions toward ordinary people were feared and unpredictable. We learn, therefore, in Luke's birth narratives that Rome is in control, or thinks it is: The emperor decrees a census that will bring an expectant mother and her husband to a distant village, searching for shelter. We hear from Matthew's Gospel of the duplicitous Herod, calling himself "King of the Jews" while he betrays the people, bringing death to Rachel's children and making refugees of the holy family.

These same intractable forces of evil will appear again and converge in a conspiracy of death because they can no longer tolerate this Jesus who preaches an end to tyranny and the coming of God's own kingdom among us. God's power for life triumphs: The baby Jesus is born in improbable circumstances and grows up to be anointed by God at his baptism. The crucified Jesus is raised from death and brought to God's right hand, a victory of life for earth and all its creatures. The story is seamless and cannot be segmented; the reason for this season of joy is God's gift of life, given to us by the power we know through Jesus' resurrection. We are always Advent people, living lives filled with light and hope even in times of turmoil and trouble because we follow the One whom death could not defeat and who comes now and will come again bringing life to all.

In the old English carol that begins "tomorrow shall be my dancing day," the dancer is Jesus, calling the world, his true love to dance his story with him. The early stanzas invoke images of the Incarnation, the "Word made flesh," and tell of Jesus' birth "betwixt an ox and a simple poor ass." But the *Oxford Book of English Carols* goes on to record many more stanzas of this carol, the final ones not often heard on our Christmas albums. The song is completed with Jesus' crucifixion and the "dancing day" of the Resurrection. The joy of the Resurrection authorizes the joy of Christmas. Easter dancing and Christmas dancing are one. "This have I done for my true love."

The prayers in this book are written to reflect the tradition, but do so in contemporary language and with an awareness of the situation and concerns of modern worshipers. They are based on the Scriptures that have for generations shaped our worship during Advent and Christmas. I have relied for the most part on the readings from the *Revised Common Lectionary*, but the themes and emphases of the prayers are ones we hold in common, and the biblical texts are often the ones that will be chosen in this season by those who do not usually follow the lectionary.

There are two special services of celebration included for Advent and three for Christmas. These are not intended to replace traditional services already in place, but to offer smaller congregations and others who wish to extend their celebrations ideas for planning that require fewer resources and involve lay people, including youth and children, in leadership. I have also tried in the Sunday celebrations to be aware of the need for new ideas that do not require elaborate equipment or specialized staff. For the Sundays in this book, for example, the Acts of Praise are stories or responsive readings, sometimes with congregational singing, that can be used in almost any church situation, including worship at church meetings and parties. The Sunday prayers given here follow the order of worship used in many Presbyterian, Methodist, and United Church of Christ congregations.

Additional resources include prayers for household worship and small groups, and ideas for programs and celebrations at church-related institutions such as residential care facilities. Four small-group study sessions are provided for Advent, and in the Christmas section, suggestions for worship and for further study are found in the section called "The Twelve Days of Christmas." I learned about the significance of celebrating the Twelve Days—along with many other things—from Virginia Sloyan when we were colleagues at The Liturgical Conference, and I am thankful for all that she taught me and especially for her lasting friendship.

Finally, I hope that the resources in this book encourage worship at gatherings of families and friends that occur during Advent and Christmas. On these occasions as well as meal times or times around the Christmas tree, prayer and the reading or telling of the stories from Scripture help us hear and remember the story of Jesus Christ above the din of competing stories in our culture.

When our children were growing up, we lived in a house on the campus of Eden Theological Seminary in St. Louis. From 1977 to 1989, on the second Sunday of Advent every year, a group of friends gathered at our home for potluck. Before dinner we all crowded into the living room for Advent prayers, singing, and the lighting of the Advent wreath. There were usually about twenty-five of us, with an age range of eight months to eighty years, and we always marked significant events in our lives as well as happenings in the wider world. We celebrate and remember those times of Advent prayer together, and today I am deeply grateful to these friends. Their joy at the Advent celebrations and their continuing encouragement have stayed with me through the writing of this book.

PART ONE

Advent

Introduction

"Joy of Heaven, to Earth Come Down"

C ome, Lord Jesus, be our guest." The familiar table grace many of us learned as children is also an Advent prayer, full of hope and longing. In Advent, although we are preparing for the annual Christmas commemoration of Jesus' birth long ago in Bethlehem, we are also keenly aware of the need for Jesus to come again, bringing the fullness of peace and justice with his promised reign. The story we tell begins with the God of Israel, who saw the suffering of the people enslaved by Pharaoh and came down to deliver them. This same God sees the suffering of people today and will come again, bringing freedom from death and sin. The coming of Jesus promises life to all creation and assures victory over all God's enemies.

The challenge we face as worship planners is to tell the Advent story and be heard when we are surrounded by a multitude of competing stories, distracting and confusing us. The story of the God who comes is distorted from all sides. It is sometimes dismissed by those who place their faith in humanity's ability to save itself and, on the other hand, sometimes distorted by those who paint a picture of Jesus for their own purposes that is not true to the Bible. The best-selling novels in the *Left Behind* series, in which Jesus returns with a vengeful, unmerciful hand, are one example of the latter misinterpretation.

The Jesus whose coming we proclaim in Advent is the Joy of Heaven, God's love sent to earth for the sake of all creation. Those who see Jesus as an instrument of suffering to be visited on the unenlightened have not read the Bible carefully. God sent Jesus not to condemn but to save the world (John 3:17). God sent Jesus to break down the dividing wall, to draw all people unto him. For this reason the Advent scriptures are a source of hope, not fear. We have God's word that "the light has come into the world" (John 3:19). The true light, sent from God, will not be overcome.

By proclaiming that Jesus is love, we are not falling into the trap of sentimentality that often overtakes the season. Jesus' love demands truth and action. We are held accountable for the response we make to Jesus' self-giving love, and the Advent scriptures make that clear. John the Baptist's preaching calls us to wake up and repent, as do the prophets and the Gospel writers, who had Christ's return at the end of the age on their minds. There is wailing and gnashing of teeth already today; and much of it is a consequence of human greed, selfishness, and carelessness with the stewardship of God's good creation. But we are encouraged to repent, give up foolish and destructive lifestyles, turn away from all distractions. We are invited to join the community of love and turn to life in the light of God's favor. All of this is part of the Advent story; and what's more, even in our hopelessness and fear, we are offered the power to turn back to God who is already coming toward us, running down the highway like a loving parent with open and forgiving arms.

The story we tell during Advent unfolds through the words and actions of the supporting cast: John the Baptist, God's messenger and the forerunner of Jesus; John's parents, Elizabeth and Zechariah, who sing of the Savior to come; the angel Gabriel, who appears with startling news; Mary, the willing servant of the Lord; and Joseph, the courageous helper and implementer of God's strange directives. Throughout the telling of the story, the Hebrew prophets reappear, they who learned, even in the desolation of exile, to read the signs of hope for God's promised reign and foresaw the coming of a just ruler, springing from the throne of David.

Advent Ventures and Adventures

Every one likes to start out on an adventure, and Advent becomes an adventure when a worshiping community is willing to venture something, to take risks. Risk taking in worship means learning to praise the God who takes incredible risks on our behalf. To praise this God we will take seriously the first Christmas greeting of the angels: "Do not be afraid!" Do not be afraid of the newness God promises. Do not be afraid to speak God's word of justice to a society that "tramples on the needy." Do not be afraid to proclaim the One who brings light and life even in places where death is expected and life treated carelessly.

The story can be told only if we know it and love it with all our hearts, and if we are willing to live it as a community. John the Baptist is an example whose story we hear again in Advent. He was a man sent from God who chose to live in a way that was completely in tune with God's word, even if that meant living a life contrary to the dominant culture of his time. The prophets too had sight of God's new creation, leading them to speak of God's harmonious mountain, though they lived in a deep ravine of conflict. We also know that God's reign was envisioned in ancient Hebrew worship; the prayers and songs in the book of Psalms encourage us to work for the time when "righteousness and peace will kiss each other" (Psalm 85:10). Living as if God's new order has already begun is a risk, but it is what we are called to wake up and do. Our liturgy during Advent can help give us ways to tell our story that invite us to remember the events past but at the same time participate now in the newness Jesus brings.

Advent is a participatory adventure: lighting candles, singing hymns, praying together, acting out the stories, and above all, bringing newness and light into lives that are dominated by the shadow of death. "Soon and very soon," the King is coming to meet us. This is the conviction of our Advent worship. We know that Jesus came to a poor and oppressed people two thousand years ago in Bethlehem, a coming that changed the world. Every year during Advent we wait eagerly for the celebration of Jesus' birth at Christmas. We are joyful in the assurance his past coming gives us for God's promised future when Jesus will come again to reign in glory. We are also joyful because we know that Jesus comes to us now: in the power of the Spirit, in our prayer and praise, through the community of Jesus' friends, in the faces of suffering people, and in everyday ways we can't even anticipate.

Advent begins with the announcement of God's future reign, the "new creation," and ends with the assurance that God's reign has already begun in Jesus. But also each Sunday's worship moves us from quiet reflection on God's promises to rejoicing in God's great gift. Sunday worship in our tradition is based on our belief that every Sunday is a "little Easter"; that is, we worship on Sunday because Jesus rose from the dead on the first day of the week, and every Sunday we gather to remember and praise God for Jesus' resurrection. Advent in particular is the celebration of the promise that Christ will bring an end to all that is contrary to the ways of God, and finally to death itself. The Advent scriptures that announce the end time are therefore a source of joy because we know that our future is secured by God, the Alpha and Omega, the beginning and the end.

Praying for Jesus' Coming

The book of Revelation is written by a believer named John, exiled to the island of Patmos, who, in his loneliness, remembered pieces of liturgy from his beloved community. In his desperate situation the promise of Christ's ultimate victory over evil was John's source of hope. He heard the invitation "Let everyone who is thirsty come . . . take the water of life as a gift." He prayed the familiar prayers in communion with the church he was separated from across the sea: "'Surely I am coming soon.' Amen. Come, Lord Jesus!" (Revelation 22:17, 20). The power of this prayer is still evident today, and it is our Advent prayer.

Prayer at communal worship, prayer in small groups, and prayer in the family is at the heart of our Advent celebration. Even social gatherings in our homes during Advent can be transformed by including prayers and lighting candles. In our time of fear and uncertainty, our Advent hymns and prayers pour out all our longing for God's just reign, like water on a thirsty ground.

My hope in this book is to provide some suggestions and models for Advent prayers, beginning with the Sundays of Advent. In addition to the Sunday prayers, I have proposed two other services of worship. One is a simple service of prayers, readings, and hymns for an Advent Sunday gathering to prepare the church building for Christmas. This service can be planned and led by the youth group or a Sunday school class. I have also included a service of hope and healing to be offered in recognition of the grief and hopelessness some families and individuals feel at this time of the year. Many congregations have found such a service helpful to the community as a whole, for it gives us the opportunity to surround and support those who are ill or have experienced loss or separation from loved ones.

A resource for study groups and classes who meet during Advent is also in this section and is given in the context of prayer. The four-week study outline with discussion questions is based on Scripture readings and Christmas carols.

And we will consider the children. Children are often more visible during Sunday morning worship for Advent than at other times of the year, and their participation is a blessing. They teach us how to be expectant. They may be asked to light the candles, lead prayers, take up the offering, and sing the Advent songs. There are sometimes opportunities to include them in biblical dramas, choral readings, and dance. But children need to learn to pray at home. For this reason, I have included a section of prayers for use by households or small groups; and to encourage more storytelling as part of worship, I have suggested four stories for Advent.

The Advent stories in this section can be used in a variety of ways in addition to telling them at home. The stories are brief and can serve as the narration for a service of Advent lessons and carols. They could also be used with music as the basis for an Advent program at church or in a nursing center, perhaps asking children to improvise a dance or pantomime that reflects the story. They are all biblical stories, told to encourage listeners of all ages to hear once again the story behind the story of Jesus' birth. Without these stories, we—like children who have an unrealistic wish list derived from the toy store—may not know what to expect and hope for at Christmas. Together let us enter the season of expecting the Joy of Heaven, who has decided to make his home with us. In this season of light and hope, we look for God to finish the new creation, and we welcome Jesus again into our lives.

Jesus, thou art all compassion,
pure, unbounded love thou art. . . .
fix in us thy humble dwelling. . . .
enter every trembling heart.
(Charles Wesley, "Love Divine, All Loves Excelling," 1740)

Sunday Prayers and Liturgies

First Sunday of Advent

We are waiting—not always patiently, and certainly not in idleness—for the coming of Jesus Christ. We remember his birth long ago in Bethlehem. We invite him into our lives now. We look for his coming again in clouds of glory to bring all peoples into his reign of peace. Let us enter once more into the great adventure of Advent.

Greeting

The grace of God, the love of Jesus Christ,
and the communion of the Holy Spirit be with us now and always.
Praise God's holy name.

God's name be praised.

Call to Worship

Come, let us go in gladness to the house of the Lord.

**Let us call on the name of the Lord our God,
who does awesome deeds we do not expect.**

To you, O Lord, we lift up our souls.
In you we trust, O our God.

Let your face shine, O God; save and restore us.
For you we will wait all day long.
(based on Psalms 25, 122, 80; Isaiah 64)

Opening Prayer

Merciful God, you are our light and our hope:
Come to us in our worry and distress; drive away our fear.
Come to rule the world with your truth and grace;
guide the nations to reflect the glories of your justice and love.
Make us ready to observe the birth of the Prince of Peace,
that we may work always for the coming of your perfect peace.
In the name of Christ our Savior. **Amen.**

The Lighting of the Advent Candle

Voice 1:
On each Sunday of Advent, we light a new candle, a sign of hope
in a world full of shadows. When all four candles are burning
brightly, we will know that it is time to begin the Christmas feast
of lights. We want to be ready to welcome the Light of the World
into our lives.

Response:
Come, let us walk in the light of the LORD!

Voice 2 (read while the candle is being lighted):
Let this light shine so that we may remember to bring the light of
Jesus' presence to all people. "While you have the light, believe in
the light, so that you may become children of light." *(John 12:36)*

Response:
Come, let us walk in the light of the LORD!

(Sung or spoken as a prayer)
Come thou long expected Jesus,
born to set thy people free;
from our fears and sins release us,
let us find our rest in thee.
Israel's strength and consolation,

14

hope of all the earth thou art;
dear desire of every nation,
joy of every longing heart. *(Charles Wesley)*

Response:
Come, let us walk in the light of the LORD! *(Isaiah 2:5)*

Call to Confession

God knows the measure of the tears we drink, the weight of the burdens we bear. But God gives us life when we call on God's name. Let us lay our tears and our burdens before God.

(based on Psalm 80)

Prayer of Confession

You have promised, O Lord,
to forget your anger and remember our sins no more.
We confess that we have not always walked in your paths
 or trusted your promises.
We look for security in the wrong places,
 and fail to lean on your mighty, outstretched arm.
We are distracted by worries and possessions
 and do not see the favor of your grace surrounding us.
We desire the things that will not last
 and neglect the abundant gifts of your Spirit.
Wake us up to your goodness and mercy:
hear us; forgive us; restore us.
In Jesus' name. Amen.

Words of Assurance

Now consider this: we are all God's people. God will lead us like a flock, open for us streams of water in the desert, and give us life. Thanks be to God!

Acts of Praise *In Praise of Jesus Christ: A Reading and Hymn*

Leader:
Let us pray.

God of glory and might, you sent Jesus Christ your Son to live and die with us; you raised him from the dead and gave him a name that is above every name: Grant us courage to live in the hope of his coming again to rule the world in peace and justice. We pray with thanksgiving for Jesus' coming and with praise for his holy name. **Amen.**

Reader:
"Then they will see 'the Son of Man coming in clouds' with great power and glory. Then he will send out the angels, and gather his elect from the four winds, from the ends of the earth to the ends of heaven." *(Mark 13:26-27)*

(Read or sung by congregation, choir, or soloist)
Lo, he comes with clouds descending,
once for favored sinners slain;
thousand, thousand saints attending
swell the triumph of his train,
Hallelujah! Hallelujah! Hallelujah!
God appears on earth to reign.

Reader:
"To him who loves us and freed us from our sins by his blood,
. . . to him be glory and dominion for ever and ever.
Look! He is coming with the clouds;
every eye will see him,
even those who pierced him;
and on his account all the tribes of the earth will wail.
So it is to be. Amen." *(Revelation 1:5b-7)*

(Read or sung by congregation, choir, or soloist)
The dear tokens of his passion
still his dazzling body bears;
cause of endless exultation
to his ransomed worshipers;
with what rapture, with what rapture, with what rapture,
gaze we on those glorious scars!

Reader:
"People will faint from fear and foreboding of what is coming upon the world, for the powers of the heavens will be shaken. Then they will see 'the Son of Man coming in a cloud' with power and great glory. Now when these things begin to take place, stand up and raise your heads, because your redemption is drawing near." *(Luke 21:26-28)*

(Read or sung by congregation, choir, or soloist)
Yes, Amen! Let all adore thee,
high on thy eternal throne;
Savior, take the power and glory,
claim the kingdom for thine own.
Hallelujah! Hallelujah! Hallelujah!
Everlasting God, come down!
(Charles Wesley, 1758)

Reader:
"'I am the Alpha and the Omega,' says the Lord God, 'who is and who was and who is to come, the Almighty.'" *(Revelation 1:8)*

Prayer for Illumination

God our Creator,
we are the work of your hand; you have molded us.
Now enrich us in speech and knowledge of every kind.
Lead us in your truth and teach us,
for you are the God of our salvation
and we will wait for you.
Prepare us with all spiritual gifts
for the revealing of our Lord Jesus Christ,
our Savior and Friend. **Amen.**
(based on Isaiah 64:1-9 and 1 Corinthians 1:3-9)

Prayer of Thanksgiving after the Offering

How can we thank you enough, O God,
for all the joy we feel before you?
Increase our gifts
that we may abound and increase

17

in love for one another and for all
as we abound in love for you.
In Jesus' name. Amen. *(based on 1 Thessalonians 3:9-13)*

Prayers of Intercession and Thanksgiving

God of Israel, good and upright Judge, Lover of justice:
Come to rule over all the earth with mercy and truth.
Jesus Christ, holy Child of Bethlehem, Word made flesh:
Open wide the door of your home among us and bring us in.
Holy Spirit, sent from God, our Advocate and Comforter:
Tear open the heavens and come down.

Lord, make us ready to receive you.

O come to us, abide with us, our Lord Emmanuel!

You have given us, great God, evidence of your awesome power:
Teach us to trust in you alone
and not to fear what the future holds.
You have shown us the tireless love of a longing parent:
Guide us in the way of your beloved Son, our brother Jesus Christ.
Grant us grace to welcome the gift you gave us:
a righteous Branch, springing up from David
to carry out justice and goodness in the land.
Give us courage to look for Christ's coming
among clouds of glory,
and to live now as citizens of Christ's reign,
who know the honor of his name.

Lord, make us ready to receive you.

O come to us, abide with us, our Lord Emmanuel!

Come, loving God; make your presence known to us;
we look for the light of your face.
Come to those who are sick and those in distress;
we wait for your healing touch.
Come to victims of violence and fear;
we cry out for your comfort and your hope.

Come to those who work for peace;
we long to turn our swords into plowshares.
Come to all earth's children;
we ask you to call us by our names.

Lord, make us ready to receive you.

O come to us, abide with us, our Lord Emmanuel!

Merciful God,
no one but you knows the day or the hour of Christ's coming;
Keep us ever watchful, doing your work,
learning the things that make for peace.
Give us the joy of receiving Jesus when we least expect him;
open our lives to his coming in many ways through all our days;
make us glad in the hope of Christ's glorious coming
in your good time.
Accept our praise and thanksgiving for your gift of light and life,
through Jesus Christ, our Savior. Amen.

Commission and Blessing

Grace to you and peace from God who loves us. God is faithful
and calls us into communion with Jesus Christ our Lord through
the power of the Holy Spirit.

For the sake of all our relatives and friends, I will say: "Peace be
with you. Amen."

Let all the people say: **"Peace be with you. Amen."**

Second Sunday of Advent

One adventure of Advent is learning to live a new way, reflecting our belief that Jesus' reign has already begun. John the Baptist was the forerunner, showing us that belonging to Jesus makes a difference in the way we choose to live. Not many of us want to retreat like John to the wilderness and eat off the land; but our society's values, including its preoccupation with possessions (the commercialization of Christmas is one example) often make us ill at ease with the ways of popular culture. We are called by our worship to honor God who sets us apart and invites us to be God's holy people. Jesus' coming makes possible a new creation.

Greeting

May the God of hope fill you with all joy and peace in believing, so that you may abound in hope by the power of the Holy Spirit. *(Romans 15:13)*

Lift up your hearts.

We lift them up to the Lord.

Call to Worship

A voice cries out:
"In the wilderness prepare the way of the LORD,
make straight a highway in the desert for our God."

Blessed be the Lord God of Israel
who has looked on us with favor and redeemed us.

Proclaim the name of Jesus Christ, our redeemer,
and sing praises to his name.

Praise the Lord;
let all the people praise God's holy name.
(based on Isaiah 40:3; Luke 1:68; Romans 15:9-11)

Opening Prayer

Lord God of Israel, who alone does wondrous things,
we are waiting and longing for the day
when steadfast love and faithfulness will meet;
when justice and peace will kiss each other;
We know that with you one day is like a thousand years
and that your patience is our salvation:
come suddenly; show us the mercy promised to our ancestors.
At your coming, let us be found by you at peace.
In Jesus' name. **Amen.**
(based on Psalm 85:10; Malachi 3:1; Luke 1:72; 2 Peter 3:8, 14)

The Lighting of the Advent Candles

Voice 1:
On the second Sunday of Advent, we light two candles to show
that the church joyfully awaits the coming of its Savior, who
enlightens our hearts and scatters the shadows of fear and doubt.
We pray that God will bless our lighting of these candles so that
we may reflect the splendor of Christ, our Light.

Response:
Come, Lord Jesus, and turn us toward your light.

Voice 2 (read while the candles are being lighted):
If we walk in the light as God is in the light,
we have fellowship with one another,
and the blood of Jesus, God's Son, cleanses us from all sin.
(1 John 1:7, adapted)

Response:
Come, Lord Jesus, and turn us toward your light.

(Sung or spoken as a prayer)
Come down to us like showers upon the fruitful earth;
love, joy, and hope, like flowers spring in your path to birth.
Before you on the mountains, shall peace the herald, go,
and righteousness, in fountains, from hill to valley flow.
*("Hail to the Lord's Anointed," James Montgomery, Psalm 72,
altered)*

Response:
Come, Lord Jesus, and turn us toward your light.

Call to Confession

John the Baptist proclaimed a baptism of repentance, of turning away from sin and seeking God's favor. Let us also confess our sins and turn again toward the light of the One greater than John, Jesus of Nazareth, whose coming John announced.

Prayer of Confession

God, our Judge and our Guide,
you sent your messenger John
to cry out to those who fail to heed your word.
Give us hearts tuned to your voice
and songs to sing your praise.
Forgive us for following crooked paths,
and put us on your straight highway.
Be our companion through the valleys
and keep us from stumbling in rough places.
Make a way for us in the wildernesses of our distress.
Help us to determine what is best
so that at Christ's coming we may be pure and blameless,
for the glory and praise of God. Amen.

Words of Assurance

The Lord speaks tenderly to us,
for Jesus Christ has paid the penalty for our sins.
"The glory of the Lord shall be revealed,
and all people shall see it together,
for the mouth of the Lord has spoken." *(Isaiah 40:5)*
Thanks be to God!

Acts of Praise   **Hope of the World: A Reading and Hymn**

Leader:
Jesus, the anointed One, comes
"to bring good news to the poor, . . .
to proclaim release to the captives

and recovery of sight to the blind,
to let the oppressed go free,
to proclaim the year of the Lord's favor." *(Luke 4:18-19)*

Like John the Baptist, we are called to prepare the way for Jesus' coming. With God's help, we will live faithful lives, working toward the day when righteousness shall flourish and peace abound.

Reader 1:
"Let me hear what God the LORD will speak,
    for God will speak peace to the people,
    to the faithful, to those who turn to God in their hearts.
Surely salvation is at hand for those who fear God,
    that the glory of the LORD may dwell in our land."
(based on Psalm 85:8-9)

(Read or sung by congregation, choir, or soloist)
Hail to the Lord's Anointed, great David's greater Son!
Hail in the time appointed, his reign on earth begun!
He comes to break oppression, to set the captive free;
to take away transgression and rule in equity.

Reader 2:
"The wolf shall live with the lamb,
and the leopard shall lie down with the kid,
the calf and the lion and the fatling together,
and a little child shall lead them. . . .
They will not hurt or destroy
on all my holy mountain;
for the earth will be full of the knowledge of the LORD
as the waters cover the sea." *(Isaiah 11:6, 9)*

(Read or sung by congregation, choir, or soloist)
He comes with succor speedy to those who suffer wrong;
to help the poor and needy, and bid the weak be strong;
to give them songs for sighing, their darkness turn to light,
whose souls, condemned and dying, are precious in his sight.

Reader 3:
"By the tender mercy of our God,
the dawn from on high will break upon us,
to give light to those who sit in darkness
and in the shadow of death,
to guide our feet into the way of peace." *(Luke 1:78-79)*

(Read or sung by congregation, choir, or soloist)
To him shall prayer unceasing and daily vows ascend;
his kingdom still increasing, a kingdom without end.
The tide of time shall never his covenant remove;
his name shall stand forever; that name to us is love.
(James Montgomery)

Leader:
According to God's promise, we wait for new heavens and a new earth. While we wait, let us work now for a place where justice, goodness, and mercy are at home. The peace of Christ is with us always.

Prayer for Illumination

God of wisdom,
we know that you have begun a good work in us
and will bring it to completion:
Fill us with your knowledge, Lord,
as the waters cover the sea.
Grant us love that overflows;
give us insight to know what is best
and work to bring in the harvest of goodness
that comes through Jesus Christ
for the glory and praise of God. **Amen.**
(based on Isaiah 11:9; Philippians 1:3-11)

Prayer of Thanksgiving after the Offering

Gracious God, you give us what is good;
our land yields prosperity, and we are thankful:
May our gifts help your good harvest spread to all.
Remind us of your promise to deliver the needy;

lead us to bring your justice to the poor
so that our offering may be pleasing to you.
In Jesus' name. Amen.

Prayers of Intercession and Thanksgiving

Holy God, hope of longing people everywhere,
you have made your home with us
and promised faithfulness that will spring up from the ground,
righteousness that will look down from the sky:
Bring quickly the day of Christ's coming to reign in peace.

**Christ, we long for you; Christ, we look for you;
Christ, we pray for you.**

Comfort your people: those who are afraid,
those who are lonely, those who grieve,
and those who are sick.
Protect us with your strong arm from all our enemies.
Find us and gather us in your arms like a mother.
Lead us like a shepherd to healing streams.
Encourage us to live in harmony with one another
and to give the compassion of Christ Jesus.

**Christ, we long for you; Christ, we look for you;
Christ, we pray for you.**

Guide rulers and all who hold elected office.
Give them your justice; may they judge with equity,
defend the cause of the poor,
and bring deliverance to the needy.
Prepare the powerful for the time when
"a little child shall lead them." *(Isaiah 11: 6c)*
Reveal your glory to all nations
and bring us to your reign of truth.

**Christ, we long for you;
Christ, we look for you;
Christ, we pray for you.**

We give you thanks for the welcome of Christ
that brings us joyfully to your table.
Teach us with one voice to praise your name
as we wait for Christ's return.
Make us your heralds of peace, proclaiming with gladness:
"Every valley shall be lifted up,
and every mountain and hill be made low." *(Isaiah 40:4)*
In the name of Christ.

Thanks be to God. Amen.

Commission and Blessing

Therefore, beloved, as our brother Paul wrote to you,
according to the wisdom given to him:
While you are waiting for the coming of Jesus Christ,
work to be found by him at peace,
without spot or blemish,
always thankful for the patience of our Lord.
Let us also with one voice
glorify the God and Father of our Lord Jesus Christ.
(based on 2 Peter 3:14-15a)

The peace of Christ be with you.

And also with you. Amen.

Third Sunday of Advent

A *re you the one who is to come, or are we to wait for another?"*
This is the question the imprisoned John the Baptist sent his
disciples to ask Jesus (Matthew 11:3). Jesus, we read in the

Scriptures, was born in an animal stall, ate with sinners, died a humil-
iating death, and was raised by God in an act of life-giving power that
defies explanation. Sometimes we, like the people of Jesus' day, want
to look for a savior who is a little more reasonable, more socially
acceptable, more in tune with the times. But in this adventure of
Advent we are asked to expect the unexpected. Jesus' coming brings
to the table the poor, the outcasts, and all in need of healing. Those
whose voices once were silenced will sing God's praise.

Greeting

> Rejoice in the Lord always; again I will say, "Rejoice."
> Let us pray without ceasing, give thanks in all circumstances,
> and do the will of God in Christ Jesus for us.
> The coming of the Lord is near.
>> *(based on Philippians 4:4-5; 1 Thessalonians 5:16-24)*
> Praise God's holy name.
>
> **God's name be praised.**

Call to Worship

> Sing praises to the LORD, who has done gloriously:
> Let God's deeds be known in all the earth.
>
> **Shout aloud and sing for joy,**
> **for great in your midst is the Holy One of Israel.**
>
> As the earth brings forth its shoots,
> and as what is sown springs up in a garden,
> so the LORD will cause righteousness and praise
> to spring up before all nations.
>
> **We will greatly rejoice in the LORD,**
> **we will praise God with our whole being.**
>> *(based on Isaiah 12:5-6; 61:10a, 11-12)*

Opening Prayer

> God of peace, when your Son Jesus was born of Mary,
> tyrants ruled, and the people were afraid.

But you love justice;
you bring your peace in the midst of great trouble and strife.
Free us from fear; bring us to your joy.
Hear our prayers and accept our thanksgiving.
Make us ready for the coming of Christ Jesus, our Lord,
in whose name we pray. **Amen.**

The Lighting of the Advent Candles

Voice 1:
On the third Sunday of Advent, we light three candles. Our hope
grows stronger, and our joy grows brighter as we prepare to celebrate Christ's coming. We remember also in this time of shadows
those whose tears still water the ground with sadness, and we pray
that God will bring all people home with shouts of joy.

Response:
Come, Lord Jesus.
In your light we will trust and not be afraid.

Voice 2: (read while the candles are being lighted):
In God's promised new heaven and new earth:
"The city has no need of sun or moon to shine on it,
for the glory of God is its light, and its lamp is the Lamb.
The nations will walk by its light,
and the kings of the earth will bring their glory into it."
(Revelation 21:23-24)

Response:
Come, Lord Jesus.
In your light we will trust and not be afraid.

(Sung or spoken as a prayer)
O come, O come, Emmanuel, and ransom captive Israel,
that mourns in lonely exile here until the Son of God appear.
Rejoice! Rejoice! Emmanuel shall come to thee, O Israel.
(9th-century Latin)

Response:
Come, Lord Jesus.
In your light we will trust and not be afraid.

Call to Confession

Crowds came to God's messenger, the man called John, and asked him what they should do. "Share whatever you have," he said. John's words call us to show by our lives that we have turned toward God and live in a community of love. Let us bring before God our concerns for our life together.

Prayer of Confession

God of love,
We have not always used our gifts for the common good:
  we have been impatient;
  we have grumbled against one another;
  we have often failed to hold fast to what is true;
  we have neglected to share all we have with those in need.
Restore us and make us instruments of your peace.
Keep us mindful of our baptism with your Holy Spirit
into the communion of Christ Jesus.
In Christ's name we pray. Amen.

Words of Assurance

God who is faithful will hear and forgive us. "And the peace of God, which surpasses all understanding, will guard your hearts and your minds in Christ Jesus." *(Philippians 4:7)*

Acts of Praise   **"Are You the One Who Is to Come?"**
                          A Reading

Leader:
Who is this Jesus whose coming we are looking for and longing for? A thousand years ago our ancestors in the church had a custom during the final days of Advent to help them think about this question. They would sing a series of prayers—one prayer on each of seven days—that focused on Jesus as God's promised Messiah. Each prayer showed them something more about Jesus. Let us now listen to some verses of scripture to remind us of the gifts Jesus brings. We will respond by singing stanzas of the familiar Advent hymn "O Come, O Come, Emmanuel," which was written from these ancient prayers.

Reader 1:
But God chose what is foolish in the world to shame the wise; God chose what is weak in the world to shame the strong; God chose what is low and despised in the world, things that are not, to reduce to nothing things that are, so that no one might boast in the presence of God. [God] is the source of your life in Christ Jesus, who became for us wisdom from God, and righteousness and sanctification and redemption. *(1 Corinthians 1:27-30)*

Response (Sung by congregation, choir, or soloist):
O come, thou Wisdom from on high,
and order all things far and nigh;
to us the path of knowledge show and cause us in her ways to go.
Rejoice! Rejoice! Emmanuel shall come to thee, O Israel.
                    (9th-century Latin, trans. Henry Sloane Coffin, 1916)

Reader 2:
This Jesus God raised up, of that all of us are witnesses, and he is therefore exalted at the right hand of God. Having received from the Father the promise of the Holy Spirit, he has poured out this Spirit so that you both see and hear. For David says in the psalms, "The Lord said to my Lord, 'Sit at my right hand, until I make your enemies your footstool.'" Therefore we know with certainty that God has made Jesus both Lord and Messiah.
                    (based on Acts 2:32-36a)

Response:
O Come, O come, great Lord of might,
who to thy tribes on Sinai's height
in ancient time once gave the law in cloud and majesty and awe.
Rejoice! Rejoice! Emmanuel shall come to thee, O Israel.
                    (9th-century Latin, trans. The Hymnal 1940)

Reader 3:
"It is I, Jesus, who sent my angel to you with this testimony for the churches. I am the root and the descendant of David, the bright morning star."
    The Spirit and the bride say, "Come."
    And let everyone who hears say, "Come."

And let everyone who is thirsty come.
Let anyone who wishes take the water of life as a gift.
(Revelation 22:16-17)

Response:
O come, thou Dayspring, come and cheer
our spirits by thy justice here;
disperse the gloomy clouds of night
and death's dark shadows put to flight.
Rejoice! Rejoice! Emmanuel shall come to thee, O Israel.
(9th-century Latin, trans. L. H. Stookey, 1986 and The Hymnal *1940)*

Reader 4:
But now in Christ Jesus you who once were far off have been
brought near by the blood of Christ. For he is our peace; in his
flesh he has made both groups into one and has broken down the
dividing wall, that is, the hostility between us.
(Ephesians 2:13-14)

Response:
O come, Desire of nations bind all peoples in one heart and mind.
From dust thou brought us forth to life;
deliver us from earthly strife.
Rejoice! Rejoice! Emmanuel shall come to thee, O Israel.
(9th-century Latin)

Leader:
Jesus Christ is "the Alpha and the Omega, the first and the last,
the beginning and the end" *(Revelation 22:13)*. Surely he is coming soon. "O come, O come, Emmanuel."

Prayer for Illumination

We would see Jesus, O God:
the sweet baby of Bethlehem,
but also Jesus as he heals,
brings good news to the poor,
and raises the dead.
We would see Jesus,
the crucified and risen One,

coming to us now.
Open our eyes and ears
to the Word made flesh.
In Jesus' name. **Amen.**

Prayer of Thanksgiving after the Offering

We give thanks to you, O Lord,
and call on your name.
We proclaim your deeds among the nations
by the sharing of our gifts,
for we are a people whom the Lord has blessed.
In Jesus' name. **Amen.**   *(based on Isaiah 12:4; 61:9)*

Prayers of Intercession and Thanksgiving

Loving God, Protector of the weak, Restorer of life,
you have given us streams of living water in desert places;
you have turned our tears to joy and filled us with laughter.
We sing "glory to God in the highest" for the gift of your Son.
We thank you that he came to live and die among us.
We praise you for your awesome power that raised him from the
    grave.

The Lord has done great things for us. Thanks be to God.

Merciful God, you came to stay in the world you love so much:
Make your presence known to those who endure pain and sorrow.
Strengthen weak hands, and make firm feeble knees.
Sing words of assurance to us and rejoice over us.
Give us words to say to those who are of a fearful heart:
"Be strong, do not fear! Here is your God."

The Lord has done great things for us. Thanks be to God.

Righteous God,
you made a covenant of peace with earth and its people;
you love justice and hate wrongdoing:
Clothe us with the garments of your goodness.

32

Gather all the people and free us from our limitations.
Guide the nations to the well of your salvation.
Let our praise spring up like fountains;
call us to hear and see and sing and leap for joy.

The Lord has done great things for us. Thanks be to God.

Holy is your name, O God,
and your mercy is from generation to generation.
You show us the strength of your arm and scatter the proud.
You bring down the powerful and lift up the lowly,
you fill the hungry with good things, and send the rich away
   empty.
Give us grace to be your servants,
to show your glory to the nations,
and give us voices to rejoice in God our Savior. In Jesus' name.

The Lord has done great things for us. Thanks be to God. Amen.

Commission and Blessing

Go and tell everyone what you have heard and seen concerning
Jesus. The God of peace will bless you and keep your mind and
soul and body sound and blameless at the coming of our Lord
Jesus Christ. The One who calls you is faithful and will do all of
this. *(based on 1 Thessalonians 5:23-24)*

The peace of Christ be with you.

And also with you. Amen.

Fourth Sunday of Advent

The angel Gabriel came to Mary with the joyful announcement of the coming birth of Jesus, her Son and God's Son, and Mary was perplexed. Her immediate concern was understandable, and her worries would deepen over the years. As Simeon later prophesied in the temple in her hearing, Mary's baby would grow up to be "opposed," and a sword would "pierce [Mary's] own soul too" (Luke 2:34-35). To his first words: "Greetings, favored one! The Lord is with you," Gabriel therefore adds, "Do not be afraid, Mary, for you have found favor with God" (Luke 1:28-29). The tidings of Jesus our Savior's coming is good news for an anxious world living in the shadow of death, and it is announced in the Gospels repeatedly with these words: "Do not be afraid."

Greeting

> But now thus says the LORD
>   who created you, O Jacob,
>   who formed you, O Israel:
> "Do not fear, for I have redeemed you;
>   I have called you by name, you are mine."
>   *(based on Isaiah 43:1)*

We belong to the God of Israel, the God of Mary and Joseph, the God of Jesus Christ, our Savior. Do not be afraid! The Lord is with you.

And also with you.

Call to Worship

God our Shepherd, you lead us like a flock: You are enthroned upon the cherubim: Shine forth; stir up your might and come to save us!

Restore us, O God of hosts; let your face shine, that we may be saved.

Put your hand on your chosen one,
the one you made strong for yourself.
Give us life, and we will call on your name.

**Restore us, O God of hosts;
let your face shine, that we may be saved.**
(based on Psalm 80:1-2, 7, 17-18)

Opening Prayer

Son of God, you took on human likeness
and became obedient to death:
Return to reign over the earth you love.
Savior of the nations, come.
Mary's Child, you made your home with us,
and God exalted you:
Shine with the light no night can overcome.
Savior of the nations, come.
Crucified and risen Jesus,
your name is above every name:
Bring us to the tree of life for the healing of the nations.
Savior of the nations, come.
Then shall every knee bow in heaven and on earth,
and every tongue confess that Jesus Christ is Lord,
to the glory of God. **Amen.**
*(based on Philippians 2:5-11; Revelation 22:1-5;
response: Martin Luther, "Savior of the Nations, Come")*

The Lighting of the Advent Candles

Voice 1:
Today we will light all four Advent candles. Their brightness
recalls God's glory that shone around the shepherds when they
heard the angel's first Christmas greeting: "Do not be afraid." We
pray that God's glory will reign on earth as it does in the highest
heaven.

Response:
**Come, Lord Jesus.
Shine on us, and the night will be bright as the day.**

Voice 2 (read while the candles are being lighted):
For once you lived in shadow, but now in the Lord you are light.
Live as children of light,
enjoying all that is good and right and true.
Try to find out what is pleasing to the Lord.
"Sleeper, awake! Rise from the dead,
and Christ will shine on you." *(Ephesians 5:8-14, adapted)*

Response:
Come, Lord Jesus.
Shine on us, and the night will be bright as the day.

(Sung or spoken as a prayer)
O holy Child of Bethlehem, descend to us we pray;
cast out our sin and enter in, be born in us today.
We hear the Christmas angels the great glad tidings tell;
O come to us, abide with us, our Lord Emmanuel!
(Philips Brooks, "O Little Town of Bethlehem")

Response:
Come, Lord Jesus.
Shine on us, and the night will be bright as the day.

Call to Confession

Jesus Christ became like us to free all who are held in slavery by the fear of death and sin. Because Jesus was tested through his suffering, he is able to help us as we are tested. Let us come to Jesus and see him as he is. *(based on Hebrews 2:14-18)*

Prayer of Confession

Jesus, Emmanuel, you are coming again, and we are not ready:
We meant to build a royal nursery,
but we find you in a stall.
We came to sing you festive carols,
but you listen to the song of doves.
We want to bring you food and gifts,
but you ask for our hearts and minds.
Forgive us for being distracted and dazzled by other lights.

Forgive us for false cheer when you are our only hope and joy.
Forgive us for overlooking you among the poor and outcast.
Come to us, abide with us, our Lord Emmanuel. Amen.

Words of Assurance

Isaiah reminds us of God's words to the weary, anxious people: "Do not remember the former things, or consider the things of old. I am about to do a new thing" *(Isaiah 43:18-19a)*. Jesus comes with newness of life for all. Thanks be to God.

Acts of Praise **The Birth of the Messiah Is Announced:**
A Reading for Four Voices

(The readers wear albs or choir robes; Mary and Elizabeth stand in the center, Gabriel stands at the pulpit, and the prophet at the lectern.)

Gabriel:
"Greetings favored one! The Lord is with you.
Do not be afraid, Mary, for you have found favor with God.
You will . . . bear a son. . . . He will be great
and will be called the Son of the Most High. . . .
And of his kingdom there will be no end." *(Luke 1:28, 30, 32)*

Mary:
"Here am I, the servant of the Lord;
let it be to me according to your word." *(Luke 1:38)*

Gabriel:
"Joseph, son of David, do not be afraid to take Mary as your wife,
for the child conceived in her is from the Holy Spirit.
You are to name him Jesus, for he will save his people from their sins." *(Matthew 1:20-21)*

Prophet:
All this took place to fulfill what had been spoken by the Lord:
"Look, the virgin shall conceive and bear a son,
and they shall name him Emmanuel,"
which means, 'God is with us.'" *(Matthew 1:22-23)*

37

Elizabeth:
"Blessed are you among women,
and blessed is the fruit of your womb.
And why has this happened to me,
that the mother of my Lord comes to me?
For as soon as I heard the sound of your greeting,
the child in my womb leaped for joy." *(Luke 1:42-44)*

Mary:
"My soul magnifies the Lord,
and my spirit rejoices in God my Savior,
for God has looked with favor on me, a lowly servant.
Surely, from now on all generations will call me blessed;
for the Mighty One has done great things for me,
and holy is God's name."

(based on Luke 1:46b-49;
the reader may continue through verse 55)

Prophet:
For a child has been born for us,
a son given to us;
authority rests upon his shoulders;
and he is named
Wonderful Counselor, Mighty God,
Everlasting Father, Prince of Peace. *(Isaiah 9:6)*

Hymn (Suggestions: "My Soul Gives Glory to My God,"
"To a Maid Engaged to Joseph")

Prayer for Illumination

Fill us with your Holy Sprit, O God;
give us the joy of knowing that our Lord is near.
Give us grace to discover your signs of hope
in women about to give birth; in joyful children;
in the eyes of older friends who show us the way;
in the faces of loved ones that shine like stars;
in candles lit by those who work for peace;
in your word that is a lamp to our feet.
Prepare us to receive the Hope of the world,

your Son Jesus, the Christ of great compassion,
who gives us the sign of his cross,
through which he conquers death and despair.
In the name of Christ. **Amen.**

Prayer of Thanksgiving after the Offering

Eternal and wise God,
you have increased our joy
and given us a harvest of good things.
Lead us with generous and thankful hearts
to help those in need of hope and healing,
that they may see your light shine in a land of darkness,
for the glory of Jesus Christ, now and forever. **Amen.**

Prayers of Intercession and Thanksgiving

God of life, Source of all our being,
you gave Elizabeth a child in her old age;
you chose Mary to be the mother of your Son:
With you nothing is impossible.
Come to us with your power to change and heal.
Make us new creations in Christ Jesus,
ready to reveal your grace and truth.
Help us to bring your word of peace to all the earth.
Lord, for your goodness and grace,

we give you thanks and praise.

Jesus our Brother, God's own Son,
you came to earth a baby, with hunger and tears;
you lived our life and died our death;
you endured all that we endure;
and by the power of your resurrection, you will help us.
Bring your light to those in the shadow of death.
Bring your hope to those in despair.
Bring your peace to those in trouble of any kind.
Lord, for your goodness and grace,

we give you thanks and praise.

Holy Spirit, ever present Comforter and Guide:
Fill us with your love; give us joy and strength
that our offering of thanks may be pleasing to God.
Bless our celebration of Christ's gracious coming;
give us songs of praise that we may sing like the angels:
"Glory to God in the highest heaven;
peace and good will to all the earth."
Lord, for your goodness and grace,

we give you thanks and praise.

We thank you, O God, that you make your home with us,
moving among your people like one who dwells in tents.
We thank you for your life-giving power to raise Jesus from the
　　dead
and bring him to reign with you and the Holy Spirit,
　　now and forever.
Give us grace to welcome the Holy Child, born to reign in us
　　today.
Give us hope that we may show your glory to the nations.
Give us joy that we may proclaim the name of Jesus, our risen
　　Savior.
Lord, for your goodness and grace,

we give you thanks and praise. Amen.

Commission and Blessing

Beloved of God, we are called to be saints. We belong to Jesus
Christ, risen from the dead, by whose grace we are made apostles,
ready to be sent into the world to bring glad tidings of great joy
to all people. "Grace to you and peace from God our Father and
the Lord Jesus Christ." *(Romans 1:7)*

The peace of Christ go with you.

And also with you.

The Hanging of the Greens

Preparing the worship space for Advent and Christmas is a joyful occasion, especially when many members of the congregation participate. Most rooms in the building will be used for worship at some time during the season—even the corridors may be the setting for caroling—and willing families, classes, or groups may be assigned responsibility for decorating various locations. The goal need not be aesthetic perfection but a coming together for fun and creativity that allows participants of all ages to say, "I helped prepare the church for Christmas." The altar guild or a similar group from the worship commission can plan, coordinate, and expedite the process, allowing for new ideas as well as seeing that much-loved traditions are continued if appropriate.

There is no pressure to complete all the decorating by the first Sunday of Advent. Adding greenery and candles week by week enhances a sense of growing anticipation. An unusual but effective idea is to build the nativity scene in stages instead of all at once. Put in place a few pieces each week, beginning on the first Sunday of Advent with the stable structure and the empty manger. A few animals are added the next Sunday; Mary and Joseph on the third Sunday; the star and angels on the fourth; and on Christmas Eve, the baby and the shepherds. The magi appear on or even after Christmas Day, and the completed crèche may remain in place through mid-January, when everyone will have time to look at it more carefully. The Christmas tree can also be decorated gradually; and if the oldest tree traditions are followed, the lights will not be turned on until Christmas Eve. Trees in churches in many places around the world traditionally remain in place at least through the Epiphany celebration.

On the first or second Sunday of Advent, plan a time immediately after the morning worship or in the late afternoon for people to gather for a simple lunch or supper and begin the decorating process. Workshops or stations are set up that can offer opportunities for participants to prepare candles, wreaths, ribbons, and other decorations. If chrismons are used to decorate the tree, consider allowing children or youth to help unpack them with proper supervision so that the adults present can talk about the symbols and tell appropriate stories. One group should be sent out to gather fresh evergreens; having some fresh, local evergreens—maybe in a container of water—is important, even if most of the decorating is done with artificial greenery. While these activities are going on, another group may well be in the kitchen baking something that smells delicious.

At the end of the work period, the entire group gathers for worship. The designated candles in the Advent wreath, which may already have been used in morning worship, may be lighted again.

Lighting an Advent wreath in a worship service is a relatively new custom with several variations, and the wreath need not be elaborate. Four candles, usually purple or red, are arranged in greenery to signify, by gradually lighting all the candles as the weeks progress, the approaching Christmas feast of lights. There is often a "Christ candle" in the center, but some traditions prefer that the Paschal candle alone represent the light of Christ. The placement of the wreath should be to the side of or below the lectern. The visual focus of the worship space at Christmas is, as throughout the year, the cross, the font, and the table. None of these symbols should be obscured in any way.

The following service is easy to prepare and may be led by the youth group or older children. The participants should be part of the planning and have time to rehearse. The readers should be chosen early, given their parts to study, and coached on good public speaking techniques.

Service of Readings and Hymns for the Hanging of the Greens

Greeting

> *Leader:*
> We thank God for the joy that surrounds us in this place,
> and we ask God's blessing as we prepare
> for the holy season of Christmas.

> *Response:*
> **I was glad when they said to me,**
> **"Let us go to the house of the Lord!"** *(Psalm 122:1)*

> *Leader:*
> Blessed is the Lord who gives us light.
> Lead the festal procession with branches
>   up to the horns of the altar. *(based on Psalm 118:27)*

Hymn (Suggestions: "Hail to the Lord's Anointed," "Prepare the Way of the Lord")

> *(The readers and other leaders enter during the hymn. Each carries greenery or a candle. During the singing, these are placed quickly in designated places.)*

First Reading **Psalm 148**

> *(The psalm may be read by two groups of readers, alternating verses, or by the whole congregation.)*

43

Psalm Prayer

God our Creator, you are praised by all the earth;
even the wind sings in the trees to praise your glory:
Teach us a new song of thanksgiving for your awesome deeds,
and bless us as we prepare your house to honor your name,
for you are with us here, and you reign in highest heaven.
In the name of Jesus, your risen Son. **Amen.**

Hymn (Suggestions: "Let All Things Now Living," "All Creatures of Our God and King")

Second Reading   **Isaiah 11:1-10**

(For two voices: Reader 1 reads vv. 1-3; Reader 2 reads vv. 4-5; Reader 1 reads vv. 6-9; Reader 2 reads vv. 10-11.)

Prayer for Peace

Loving God,
you sent your Son Jesus to break down walls that divide
    and to reconcile all people to you:
Teach us to be peacemakers and stewards of the earth.
Give us courage to share what we have with glad hearts
so that others may be sheltered, fed, and loved.
Help us to live each day filled with your grace
and in harmony with one another.
In the name of the Prince of Peace. **Amen.**

Hymn (Suggestions "How Majestic Is Your Name," "Hope of the World," "The Friendly Beasts")

Third Reading **Trees of Honor**

The Bible is full of stories about trees, from the tree in the garden of Eden to the tree of life growing on either side of the river that flows from the throne of God. Trees provide food for people and animals, shelter for birds and squirrels, and shade from the burning sun when we are tired. The leaves of the tree of life bring healing *(Revelation 22:2)*.

The Bible also talks about family trees, which help us remember the stories of our ancestors. Jesus' family tree goes back to

Jesse, the great King David's father. Jesus knew he was in the royal line of David, chosen to be God's King, a king who will bring peace, defend the cause of the poor, help those who have no helper, end oppression and violence, and reign over all the earth *(Psalm 72)*. Trees are signs of our life together as God's family.

There is still another reason that tree branches have been used to decorate houses of worship since long ago. In biblical times, people welcomed home a victorious king by placing leafy branches on the processional way for the king to ride over. The ancient Hebrews honored God in this way by carrying branches in processions to adorn "the horns of the altar" in the Temple *(Psalm 118:27)*. They wanted to show that God was their one true Ruler, and they gave thanks to God, who brings victory.

Jesus' followers honored him by placing branches in his path on the way to Jerusalem on the day we call Palm Sunday. By doing this, they were calling him God's chosen King, the King of Peace, who would be victorious over death. Trees help us remember that Jesus died for us and rose again to life.

Evergreen trees are fresh and green all year round, reminding us that Jesus comes so we might have life, always. An old legend says that the holly tree bears a flower to remind us of Jesus' goodness, a thorn to remind us of the crown of thorns, and a red berry to remind us of the blood Jesus shed. A tree provided the wood for the manger where Mary placed the newborn baby Jesus, and wood from a tree was used to make the cross.

Let us pray together that as we prepare the church for Christmas with green branches, we will prepare our hearts to receive Jesus, our Savior and Friend.

Responsive Prayer

Gracious God,
we thank you for the coming of Jesus long ago in Bethlehem,
for his willingness to become like us, to live with us,
to die for us, and to come to live with us again.
Make us ready to open our lives to his coming every day.

Come, Lord Jesus.

Help us to remember the gifts of Jesus' coming:
how he fed the hungry, healed the sick,

and freed us from fear.
Free us now to do his work.

Come, Lord Jesus.

You have promised to plant us like a tree by the riverside,
a tree with roots deep in the soil of your love:
Help us to grow and become strong and beautiful for you.

 Come, Lord Jesus.

Make our homes bright with the joy of your presence
and our churches alive with glad songs of praise for your coming.
Give us faces that shine with your light for the world to see.

 Come, Lord Jesus. Amen.

*Hymn (Suggestions: "I Want to Walk as a Child of the Light,"
"Come, Thou Long Expected Jesus")*

Offering

Leader: Let us bring to God with joy our gifts and offerings.

*(Music suggestions: "The Holly and the Ivy," "O Christmas
Tree")*

*(The offering may include a procession of children and youth car-
rying gifts of poinsettias and small evergreen plants, collected
ahead of time, to be taken to the sick or to places where the congregation engages in mission, such as hospitals, after-school programs, and soup kitchens.)*

Prayer of Thanksgiving after the Offering

Gracious God,
your creation is good, and we are thankful.
We join with the trees and hills,
the creatures of the land and sea to sing your praise.
Give us glad and generous hearts;
teach us to spread your abundant gifts to others.

Make us ready to welcome with joy
the One who came to deliver the needy.
In Jesus' name. **Amen.**

Fourth Reading **Philippians 4:4-7**

Passing of the Peace

Leader: As we await the coming of the Prince of Peace, let us joyfully greet each other with expressions of affection and peace.
May the peace of Christ go with you.

Response: **And also with you.**

Hymn (Suggestions: "Dona Nobis Pacem," "Peace Like a River")

A Service of Healing and Hope

Greeting

Leader:

In this season when we are expecting the joy of Christ's coming, we are near the time of the longest night of the year. We know that for some members of our community every night appears endless and the prospect of a new day seems dim. For all of us the troubles of the world are ever-present as we pray and watch with victims of violence, hunger, illness, and disaster, close at hand and throughout the earth. We are called therefore to gather as a whole community, surrounded by love, and listen to God's word; remember God's promises; and praise God who is the source of all light and hope.

The Lord be with you.

And also with you.

A Reading from Revelation

Then I saw a new heaven and a new earth; for the first heaven and the first earth had passed away, and the sea was no more. And I saw the holy city, the new Jerusalem, coming down out of heaven from God, prepared as a bride adorned for her husband. And I heard a loud voice from the throne saying,
   "See, the home of God is among mortals.
   God will dwell with them;
   they will be God's peoples,
   and God will be with them and will be their God.

God will wipe every tear from their eyes.
Death will be no more;
mourning and crying and pain will be no more,
for the first things have passed away."
And the one who was seated on the throne said,
"See, I am making all things new." *(based on Revelation 21:1-5)*

Hymn **"O Come, O Come, Emmanuel"**

Opening Prayer

Leader:
In this place we are sustained by the community of those who wait
for Christ's coming in the clouds. Together we know what it is to
hope, to lean on God's everlasting arms, to expect the coming of
God who will make a home for us beside the river of life. With the
assurance of God's promises, we extend the power of the community's prayer to the sick, the broken hearted, and those who sit in
the shadow of death.

Let us pray:
Come, Lord Jesus.
When we are weak, afraid, lonely, or sad,
we cannot sing of Christmas joy.
Come, Lord Jesus.
Gather us under your wings
as a mother hen shelters her chicks.
Come, Lord Jesus.
Weep with us
as you wept with Mary and Martha.
Come, Lord Jesus.
You know the cold and hunger of a stable;
now share our loneliness.
Come, Lord Jesus.
You know the power of our enemy death;
now comfort and sustain us.
Come, Lord Jesus.
Make your home with us
and share our every load.
Come, Lord Jesus.

You are the Sun of righteousness,
risen with healing in your wings.
Come, Lord Jesus.
Give us life and light through the long night
and bring us to your joy in the morning.
In your name we pray.
Come, Lord Jesus. Amen.

Hymn **"Lo, How a Rose E'er Blooming"**

Acts of Reconciliation

Leader:
I invite you now to answer God's call to be reconciled to one
another and to God. Let us put aside discord and conflict, ask for
forgiveness and make peace in the name of the Prince of peace.

Let us pray together:

God of mercy,
you hear us when we cry to you and you come to save us:
Touch us now with your healing power.
Help us to lay before you every regret and disappointment;
give us courage to bring to you our grief and pain;
Teach us to live together in love with our neighbors,
and pardon us when we have acted against your will.
Encourage us with your love;
guide our feet on the way of peace.
In the name of Jesus, the healer,
who binds all wounds and forgives our sins. Amen.

(Silent prayers)

Leader:
God, you sent Jesus to bring us life
and to be the true light of all people.
Help us to live in the light
that we may have love for each other,
peace within our hearts, and hope for your future.
Let us pray together the prayer Jesus taught us:

Our Father, who art in heaven, hallowed be thy name. . . .

The Passing of the Peace

Leader:
Christ is our peace. He breaks down the walls that divide us and makes us whole. Let us now exchange greetings and signs of peace. *(The participants greet each other with handclasps or embraces, exchanging greetings such as "The peace of Christ be with you.")*

Hymn **"Hope of the World"**

Prayers for the Sick and Sorrowing

Leader:
Let us pray now for those in our community whom we know to be sick or suffering and for those who mourn. If you know of others not already brought to our attention, you may stand and speak their names as you wish. After each petition, I will close with the words "Grant our sister or brother healing and peace. God in your mercy," and you will respond: **"Hear our prayer."**

Let us pray:

Come, long-expected Jesus,
hope of all the earth, joy of longing hearts:
You look with tender mercy on all who suffer;
you promise that death will be destroyed;
and you offer your healing balm to the sick.
Come to those whose lives are touched by sadness,
for you are all compassion; pure, unbounded love.
Keep those we love in life and death in your embrace.
Remember those whose names we bring before you;
give them the comfort of your presence
and make them whole again.
Grant our *sister/ brother Name* healing and peace.
God in your mercy,

Hear our prayer.

Grant also those we name in our hearts healing and peace.
God in your mercy,

Hear our prayer.

Release us from our fears and give us rest.
Stay with us through days of doubt and sorrow
that we may know your peace.
Keep us in your embrace while we wait for your new creation
and look for the coming of your glorious reign in all the world.
In the name of the Jesus, who rose from death to life. **Amen.**

Invitation to Anointing

Reader:
Are any among you suffering?
They should pray.
Are any cheerful?
They should sing songs of praise.
Are any among you sick?
They should call for the elders of the church
and have them pray over them,
anointing them with oil in the name of the Lord. *(James 5:13-14)*

Leader:
The act of anointing with oil, a sign of the presence of the Holy
Spirit and the care of the community, is available to all who long
for the healing touch of God's hand to still our troubled minds
and to comfort us in pain and sickness. You are all invited to come
forward and kneel in prayer. If you wish, we will anoint you and
pray with you.

*(The pastor or other pastoral leaders, such as members of the
intercessory prayer group, may lay hands on each person's head as
she or he prays and offer to anoint by touching a thumb into the
oil and making the sign of the cross on the person's forehead,
using these or similar words:)*

Name, I anoint you with oil in the name of Jesus Christ who
comes to heal the sick and the broken hearted. May the Spirit of
the living God refresh you. May Jesus come to you in your need.
May God bring you wholeness and give you peace. Amen.

Prayer after Anointing

God of glory,
your angels sang a new song on the mountains:
Send them once again to comfort us.
Help us to hear the good news they told the earth:
Emmanuel has come. "Light and life to all he brings."
Grant us grace to know Jesus as one of us,
who shared our weakness and died our death
that we may one day live with him.
We ask that even now we know your life-giving love
and walk in newness of life all our days.
Through Jesus Christ, holy Child and Savior. **Amen.**

Hymn **"There Is a Balm in Gilead"**

Psalm 80:1-7, 17-19

(The congregation reads or sings together from the psalter.)

Prayer for the Suffering of the World

(This prayer may be led by two persons alternating the petitions. New petitions can also be added to address specific situations. Candles in a votive holder may be placed on a central table for those who wish to come and light them as signs of hope at the close of the prayer.)

God of all creation,
you sent your Word to live among us.
This same Word was with you at the beginning,
and all things came into being through him.
Give us grace to honor all that you have created,
to live wisely and manage well what you have made.
Open our eyes to the carelessness that threatens the earth;
let us hear the sighs of creation for your saving grace.
Teach us to care for all living things,
as you care for us and make us your children.
Grant to the earth healing and peace.
God in your mercy,

Hear our prayer.

God of the little ones,
You sent your Son to be born as a baby,
the holy Child of Bethlehem:
Hear the cries of your children everywhere,
the homeless, the orphans, the sick, the hungry,
and those in constant danger.
Hear the cry of Rachel weeping
with grieving with mothers in all places
whose children have no chance at life.
Give us courage to see the world's trouble and need
and the will to share the abundance of your good gifts.
Grant to the suffering healing and peace.
God in your mercy,

Hear our prayer.

God of the oppressed,
Jesus, your Son, comes to release the captives,
defend the needy, and crush the oppressor:
As you showed the magi Herod's treachery,
open our eyes to powers and principalities
that use death to serve their own designs.
Make us agents of your life-giving power.
Teach us to speak truth and live with grace
in the name of Jesus, sought by all who love life.
Grant to the hopeless healing and peace.
God in your mercy,

Hear our prayer.

God of the peacemakers,
your Son was born in a country at war,
and yet he is the Prince of Peace.
Help us to see his star, the light of life,
the light of hope, the light of joy.
Free us from all pride and foolish dreams of might
and let us lean on our hope in you alone.

Free us from fears that bind us to false claims.
Give us courage to know your truth and trust your word.
We give you thanks that we have seen Jesus,
whose love will destroy the power of death.
Keep us faithful as we wait for his coming again.
Grant to the world healing and peace.
God in your mercy,

Hear our prayer. Amen.

Leader:
I invite you now to come forward and light a candle signifying your
hope in Jesus Christ, the Light of the world. As the candles are lighted,
we will enter a time of silent prayer for ourselves and for others.

*(Music may be played during the time of prayer and candle-
lighting. Suggestions: "What Child Is This?" "What Wondrous
Love Is This?" "I Wonder as I Wander," Bach's "Sheep May
Safely Graze")*

Dismissal with Blessing

Leader:
Let us go in thanksgiving for the light of Jesus,
who laid his glory aside,
became obedient to death,
and rose with healing in his wings.
May God give us courage and guide our journeys
that we may bear Jesus' gifts of love and life and hope.
The Lord bless you and keep you.
The Lord's face shine upon you.
The Lord look on you with kindness
and give you peace. **Amen.**

Singing a New Song of Cradle and Cross

Four Adult Study Sessions for Advent

During Advent we are waiting for the annual celebration of Jesus' birth and expecting Jesus' coming again to rule in peace. This time of preparation offers us the opportunity to reaffirm what we believe about Jesus, God's chosen One, and pray about his coming. As a community of faith, we are aware that the birth narratives in the Gospels are only one part of the story of Jesus' coming for our salvation. We understand, therefore, that the familiar stories of the season are precursors of Jesus' life, death, and resurrection, and reminders of God's promise that Jesus will come again. The goal of these study sessions is to look at the whole story of Jesus from the perspective of the biblical accounts of Jesus' birth.

Each session will begin with prayer and Scripture reading, followed by hymns or carols that reflect the reading. The hymns may be sung, read, or listened to on a recording, and then examined carefully by the group for their message. Each participant needs a Bible and will be asked to look up texts for reference in the discussion. Permission is given for the discussion leader to photocopy the study outline given here for limited distribution to class members. One or more participants should take responsibility for preparing additional background information on the scriptures for the week with the help of commentaries and study Bibles, and sharing what they have learned with the class. Information on the origins of the hymns can be found in a companion commentary for one of the denominational hymnals. (For example, Carlton Young's *Companion to The United Methodist Hymnal*, Abingdon Press, 1993.)

If there is a resource readily available, such as an art museum or a library with a good collection of art books, ask someone to find prints that show a variety of artistic and cultural interpretations of the Christmas story and bring them to class to add to the discussion. Participants can also be asked to bring any examples they have at home, including art on Christmas cards.

Session I

Begin with prayer, spoken and silent. Read aloud each pair of verses. Pause after reading each pair for a few moments of silent reflection. Sing, read, or listen to the hymns. Read carefully again the scripture verses. Look them up in the Bible and talk about the book and chapter they come from. What do you think they meant to the first people who heard them? How do the paired verses relate to each other? Look carefully again at the words to the hymns. Describe the subject of each stanza. What do you find surprising or puzzling about their message? Continue the discussion using the suggested questions. Close with prayer.

Opening Prayer

God of hope,
we give you thanks for the light of Christ
    that overcomes all shadows:
Strengthen us in hope and holiness
    as we wait for Christ's coming with all the saints.
Give us hearts that abound in love for each other
    and voices to sing a new song of joy and peace,
    for you have done marvelous things.
    In Jesus' name. Amen.

Scripture Verses

And the glory of the Lord shone around them. *(Luke 2:9)*

In him was life and the life was the light of all people. The light shines in darkness and the darkness has not overcome it. *(John 1:4-5)*

I saw one like a human being
   coming with the clouds of heaven. . . .
To him was given dominion
   and glory and kingship,
that all peoples, nations, and languages
   should serve him. *(Daniel 7:13-14)*

And may the Lord make you increase and abound in love for one another and for all, just as we abound in love for you. And may he so strengthen your hearts in holiness that you may be blameless before our God and Father at the coming of our Lord Jesus with all his saints. *(1 Thessalonians 3:12-13)*

Hymns "Lo, He Comes with Clouds Descending," "Lo, How a Rose E'er Blooming"

Discussion Questions

1. What images come to your mind when the Bible speaks of God's glory? How is "glory" an indicator of God's presence? Explain what you think is meant by this statement: Glory links Christmas and Easter. What do we mean by "glory" in the hymn "In the Cross of Christ I Glory"?

2. Read Daniel 7:13-14 and Isaiah 11:1-10. What images do the Hebrew prophets use to characterize God's reign? How is God's reign described in Revelation 21:1-6? According to 1 Thessalonians 3:9-13 and Romans 13:11-14, what do we need to be doing as we wait for the fullness of God's reign?

3. Read Ephesians 5:8-9 and the hymn "I Want to Walk as a Child of the Light." What do we mean when we say that Jesus is the light of the world? What does it mean for us to live as "children of the light"? What activities should congregations engage in to help "give light to those who sit in darkness and in the shadow of death" (Luke 1:79)?

4. Which advent of Jesus is described in "Lo, He Comes with Clouds Descending"? Why is this hymn appropriate for the first Sunday of Advent (see Matthew 24:29-31)? In what ways does this hymn tell the whole story of Jesus?

5. In "Lo, How a Rose E'er Blooming," what is the meaning of the lines that say Jesus is "true man yet very God . . . and

share[s] our every load"? In this hymn what do you learn about the purpose of Jesus' coming?

Closing Prayer

(Ask the group to write an Advent prayer based on Scripture, or select a hymn stanza to pray together.)

Session II

Begin with prayer, spoken and silent. Read aloud each pair of verses. Pause after reading each pair for a few moments of silent reflection. Sing, read, or listen to the hymns. Read carefully again the scripture verses. Look them up in the Bible and talk about the book and chapter they come from. What do you think they meant to the first people who heard them? How do the paired verses relate to each other? Look carefully again at the words to the hymns. Describe the subject of each stanza. What do you find surprising or puzzling about their message? Continue the discussion using the suggested questions. Close with prayer.

Opening Prayer

God of peace,
we thank you for sending Jesus, the hope of all the earth.
Give us rest; free us from worries and distractions.
Teach us your perfect love that casts out all fear.
Show us how to live at peace with one another;
rule in our hearts, now and forever.
In the name of Jesus, our joy and our strength. Amen.

Scripture Verses

"Do not be afraid; for see—I am bringing you good news of great joy for all the people." *(Luke 2:10)*

"Do not fear, for I have redeemed you;
I have called you by name, you are mine." *(Isaiah 43:1)*

They shall beat their swords into plowshares
   and their spears into pruning hooks;
nation shall not lift up sword against nation,
   neither shall they learn war any more. *(Isaiah 2:4)*

By the tender mercy of our God,
  the dawn from on high will break upon us . . .
to guide our feet into the way of peace. *(Luke 1:78-79)*

Hymns "Good Christian Friends, Rejoice," "Come, Thou Long-Expected Jesus"

Discussion Questions

1. What were people afraid of in Jesus' time? What are we afraid of today? If a child is afraid of the dark, what do we do to comfort him or her? What does God do to comfort us in our fear?
2. Read Luke 12:32-40. What reason does Jesus give the disciples for not being afraid? What do these verses tell us about preparing for Jesus' coming?
3. Read Isaiah 43:1-7. What do you think it means to be "redeemed"? Does God call you by name? Explain your answer. In what way does the church name us at our baptism? Read Romans 6:1-11. What do Jesus' death and resurrection have to do with our baptism?
4. Read Isaiah 9:6 and Zechariah 9:9-10. What are the origins of Jesus' name, "Prince of Peace"? Read Ephesians 2:13-22. How does Jesus become our peace (v. 14)? Why is "proclaiming peace" a significant part of Christmas?
5. In "Come, Thou Long-Expected Jesus," what words and ideas link Jesus to the God of Israel? From what does Jesus set us free according to this hymn? According to "Good Christian Friends, Rejoice"? In these hymns what do you learn about the purpose of Jesus' coming?

Closing Prayer

(Ask the group to write an Advent prayer based on Scripture, or select a hymn stanza to pray together.)

Session III

Begin with prayer, spoken and silent. Read aloud each pair of verses. Pause after reading each pair for a few moments of silent reflection. Sing, read, or listen to the hymns. Read carefully again the scripture verses. Look them up in the Bible and talk about the book and chapter they come from. What do you think they meant to the first people who heard them? How do the paired verses relate to each other? Look carefully again at the words to the hymns. Describe the subject of each stanza. What do you find surprising or puzzling about their message? Continue the discussion using the suggested questions. Close with prayer.

Opening Prayer

> God of mercy,
> we thank you that your Son became like us,
> lived and died with us, and rose again with healing wings.
> Hear the cries of your suffering people everywhere,
> and come down to help and comfort us.
> Lead us on the way to peace;
> let us reflect your light and shine with your glory and grace.
> In the name of Jesus, who comes from God. Amen.

Scripture Verses

> "Look, the virgin shall conceive and bear a son,
> and they shall name him Emmanuel." *(Matthew 1:23)*

And the Word became flesh and lived among us. *(John 1:14)*

God has come to the help of Israel, the Lord's servant, redeeming mercy. *(based on Luke 1:54)*

Then the LORD said, "I have observed the misery of my people. . . . I have heard their cry. . . . Indeed, I know their sufferings, and I have come down to deliver them from the Egyptians, and to bring them up out of that land to a good and broad land, a land flowing with milk and honey." *(Exodus 3:7-8)*

Hymns "Hark! the Herald Angels Sing," "O Come, All Ye Faithful"

Discussion Questions

1. What do you think the phrases, "Veiled in flesh the Godhead see," and "mild he lays his glory by" mean in the hymn in

"Hark! the Herald Angels Sing"? What is the purpose of Jesus' birth according to this hymn? What lines refer to the Resurrection?

2. Read Philippians 2:5-11. What do these verses tell us about Jesus' coming?

3. What do we mean when we use the theological term "the Incarnation"? What do the birth stories in Matthew 1–2 and Luke 1–2 tell us about the Incarnation? What do the Crucifixion, Resurrection, and Ascension say to us about Jesus' Incarnation? In what ways do we experience the incarnate Christ with us today?

4. Read John 1:1-18 and then read the stanza in "O Come, All Ye Faithful" that begins, "True God of true God, Light from Light eternal." How are the hymn and the Gospel reading related? What other stanza of this hymn refers to John 1:14?

5. What does Moses' encounter with God in Exodus 3:1-15 tell us about God's coming to deliver the people? What are some of the ways God comes to suffering people today?

Closing Prayer

(Ask the group to write an Advent prayer based on Scripture, or select a hymn stanza to pray together.)

Session IV

Begin with prayer, spoken and silent. Read aloud each pair of verses. Pause after reading each pair for a few moments of silent reflection. Sing, read, or listen to the hymns. Read carefully again the scripture verses. Look them up in the Bible and talk about the book and chapter they come from. What do you think they meant to the first people who heard them? How do the paired verses relate to each other? Look carefully again at the words to the hymns. Describe the subject of each stanza. What do you find surprising or puzzling about their message? Continue the discussion using the suggested questions. Close with prayer.

Opening Prayer

God of glory,
we thank you for your wondrous love of the world

that led you to send Jesus to conquer sin and sorrow.
Give us joyful songs to welcome your Son, our Savior.
Bring us now into his reign of grace and truth.
Fill our lives with hope; encourage us in peace.
Teach us your words of good news to all the earth.
In the name of Jesus, whose glory is the cross. Amen.

Scripture Verses

This will be a sign for you: you will find a child wrapped in bands of cloth and lying in a manger. *(Luke 2:12)*

They took the body of Jesus and wrapped it with the spices in linen cloths. *(John 19:40)*

"Where is the child who has been born king of the Jews?" *(Matthew 2:2)*

Pilate also had an inscription written and put on the cross. It read, "Jesus of Nazareth, the King of the Jews." *(John 19:19)*

Hymns "Joy to the World," "We Three Kings"

Discussion Questions

1. What makes "Joy to the World" a Christmas hymn even though there is no mention of the birth stories? How is the purpose of Jesus' coming, according to this hymn, addressed to individuals? To the whole earth? Read aloud Psalm 98, the text that suggested this hymn to its author.
2. Read Luke 2:25-35. How do these verses move us toward an understanding of who Jesus is and what he would do for us? What do you think Simeon's words in verses 34-35 meant to Mary? Verses 29-42 have been sung at evening prayers by Christians for centuries. Find a musical setting for this song, the *Nunc Dimittis,* by using the Scripture index in your hymnal.
3. Read Matthew 2:1-18. What political situation is the background of this story? Why was Herod threatened by a new "king of the Jews"? This story reminds us that there is death

and suffering in the midst of our Christmas joy. How do we as individuals and as a congregation respond with hope to the crises we see on the news and the suffering of persons we know?

4. What happened in the Palm Sunday story (Matthew 21:1-11) that shows Jesus' followers thought of him as God's promised King? Why was Jesus' kingship a factor in his trial before Pilate (John 19:13-19)? What are the references to Jesus' crucifixion and resurrection in "We Three Kings"? What other Christmas hymns can you think of that refer to the Crucifixion and Resurrection?

5. Summarize some of the insights and impressions made by the class during the last four weeks. What does looking at the story of Jesus, as a whole, add to our understanding of the Christmas story? What do you like about the way we celebrate Christmas in our families and as individuals? In our church community? What would you change? How does the way we celebrate Christmas affect the way we live the rest of the year?

Closing Prayer

To close the final session, sing or read a hymn that follows Jesus' life all the way from birth to resurrection. Examples: "We Would See Jesus," "Lord of the Dance," "Amen, Amen"

Household Prayers for the Weeks of Advent

Greeting

Wait for the Lord; be strong and brave
and put your hope in the Lord.

**Then the glory of the Lord will be revealed
and all people will see it together.
Thanks be to God.**

Readings

*(Choose a Scripture reading from the list on p. 68 and/or a story
from pp. 69-73.)*

*Hymn (Suggestions: "O Come, O Come Emmanuel," "Bring Forth
the Kingdom of Mercy," "Love Divine, All Loves Excelling," "O
Come, Little Children")*

Thanksgiving for Light

The Lord be with you.
And also with you.
Let us give thanks to the Lord our God.
It is right to give our thanks and praise.
We give you thanks and praise, God of all creation:
You gave us the sun that runs its course with joy,
the moon and stars to brighten the sky at night.

Break through our clouds of doubt and fear.
Wake us up to your awesome works;
teach us again that nothing is too wonderful for our God.
Make us heralds of your peace to all the earth,
bearers of your light to those who are sad and afraid.
Grant us rest this night
that we may sleep surrounded by your love.
We pray in the name of your Son, Jesus Christ,
who is the Light of the world. **Amen.**

Lighting of the Advent Wreath

"By the tender mercy of our God,
    the dawn from on high will break upon us,
to give light to those who sit in darkness and in the shadow of
    death,
    to guide our feet into the way of peace." *(Luke 1:78-79)*

Jesus said, "I am the light of the world."
    The nations will walk by this light
    and all people will see God's glory.
(spoken as the candles are lighted)

*Responsive Prayer (For additional responsive prayers, see pp. 74-
78.)*

Jesus, our Emmanuel,
    you promised to be with us in all times and places:
Come now and be our friend.
Come, Lord Jesus.
You came as a baby, born in a manger,
    and the magi called you "King":
Come to rule the world with mercy and peace.
Come, Lord Jesus.
You walked through towns and villages,
    healing the sick and feeding the hungry:
Come and show us your way of love.
Come, Lord Jesus.
God sent you to save the earth and all its people;
    your love for us led you to the cross:

Come with joy, and open wide the door to life.
Come, Lord Jesus. Amen.

Hymn (Suggestions: "Come Thou, Long-Expected Jesus," "We've a Story to Tell to the Nations," "Beautiful Savior," "O Little Town of Bethlehem")

Prayer

God of light, you have promised that you will feed us, hold us tenderly, and protect us: Guide us through each day, and lead us on the highway to your home. Come to us when we are afraid and uncertain. Bless us as we prepare to celebrate Christmas. Gather us into a community of love, ready to receive Jesus and to bring his healing and peace to the world. In Jesus' name we pray: *(Invite participants to offer prayers of their own, and pause for silent prayers.)*

Our Father in heaven, hallowed be your name . . . Amen.

May the grace of our Lord Jesus Christ,
the love of God and the communion of the Holy Spirit be with us.
O come, O come Emmanuel!

Daily Scripture Readings for Advent

First Week of Advent

Sun	Ps 24; Rev 22:16-21
Mon	Isa 2:1-5; Rom 13:11-14
Tue	Ps 122; Mt 24:36-44
Wed	Isa 64:1-9; 1 Cor 1:3-9
Thur	Ps 80:1-7, 17-19; Mk 13:24-32
Fri	Jer 33:14-16; 1 Thess 3:9-13
Sat	Ps 25:1-10; Lk 21:25-36

Second Week of Advent

Sun	Ps 96; Col 1:3-5, 11-20
Mon	Isa 11:1-10; Rom 15:4-13
Tue	Ps 72:1-7, 18-19; Mt 3:1-12
Wed	Isa 40:1-11; 2 Pet 3:8-15a
Thur	Ps 85:1-2, 8-13; Mk 1:1-8
Fri	Mal 3:1-4; Lk 1:68-79
Sat	Phil 1:3-11; Lk 3:1-6

Third Week of Advent

Sun	Phil 2:5-11; Jn 3:16-17
Mon	Isa 35:1-10; Lk 1:46-55
Tue	Jas 5:7-10; Mt 11:2-11
Wed	Isa 61:1-4, 8-11; 1 Thess 5:16-24
Thur	Ps 126; Jn 1:6-8, 19-28
Fri	Zeph 3:14-20; Phil 4:4-7
Sat	Isa 12:2-6; Lk 3:7-18

Fourth Week of Advent

Sun	Isa 9:1-7; Lk 1:26-38
Mon	2 Sam 7:1-11, 16; Rom 16:25-27
Tue	Ps 34; Lk 1:39-45
Wed	Isa 7:10-16; Rom 1:1-7
Thur	Mic 5:2-5a; Lk 1:46-55
Fri	Ps 80:1-7, 17-19; Mt 1:18-25
Sat	Heb 10:5-10; Lk 2:1-7

Four Stories for Advent

Advent 1: A Story

A long, long time ago, the people in the poor regions of Judea and Galilee near the Mediterranean Sea were conquered by the Roman army. The Roman emperor, called Caesar, appointed a king over them named Herod, but they knew he was not their real king. The king they looked for and longed for would be descended from their great King David, and he would love and honor God. Their real king would be just and kind, like a good shepherd who loves and cares for the whole flock. While they waited for this king to come, they lived in fear of the army that occupied their country. They became poorer and poorer as Caesar became richer and richer. Like many people in our world today, they were afraid of the terror around them and afraid they would not have enough food for their children. But they also had a great hope.

While they waited for the promised king, they remembered what God's prophets had told them down through the ages: "Come, let us go up to the mountain of the LORD, who will teach us to walk in God's paths. . . . God will be our judge and peacemaker, and we will study war no more" *(based on Isaiah 2:1-5)*. They had hope because they believed God's promises, and they knew that in the past God had rescued them with "awesome deeds" they did not expect *(Isaiah 64:3)*. While they waited, they prayed together prayers like this one:

Restore us, O God of hosts;

let your face shine that we may be saved.

In you, O God, is our trust.

Lead us in your truth, and teach us,

for you are the God of our salvation;

for you we wait all day long.

We are your people, O God.
You have loved us from long ago,
and you are faithful.
Come to us with your power and glory.
Bring us peace. Amen.
(based on Isaiah 64:1-9; Psalm 80; Psalm 25)

God of mercy, you have shown us your strength and your love:
Teach us to speak your words of life to those around us
and to live in the light your promises.
Give us patience to work for your reign of joy,
through your Son, our Savior Jesus Christ. Amen

Advent 2: A Story

In the faraway country where long ago the scheming King Herod ruled in the name of the Roman emperor, there lived a couple named Elizabeth and Zechariah. They had hoped and longed for a child but never had one, and now they were old. They were lonely without a child, but they were faithful to God and God blessed them.

Zechariah served as a priest in the Temple, and one day as he was burning incense and offering prayers to God for the people, an angel stood before him, giving him a dreadful fright. The angel spoke: "Do not be afraid, Zechariah, for your prayer has been heard. Your wife Elizabeth will bear you a son, and you will name him John. You will have joy and gladness, and many will rejoice at his birth" *(Luke 1:13-14)*.

Zechariah was flabbergasted. He said to the angel, "How can this be? I'm too old to become a father, and my wife is old also." The angel scolded him for doubting God's word, for Zechariah knew the stories in the Bible of God's gift of a child to Abraham and Sarah when they were old. With God nothing is impossible.

Zechariah never spoke another word until after the baby was born, and then he wrote on a tablet: "His name is John," a name that means "God gives." Once Zechariah could speak again, he sang a beautiful song to his baby boy that we still remember today. The last part of the song goes like this:

And you, child, will be called the prophet of the Most High;
    for you will go before the Lord to prepare his ways,
to give knowledge of salvation to his people

by the forgiveness of their sins.
By the tender mercy of our God,
    the dawn from on high will break upon us,
to give light to those who sit in darkness and in the shadow of
    death,
    to guide our feet into the way of peace. *(Luke 1:76-79)*

God of life, you gave to Zechariah and Elizabeth a child of hope:
Teach us to expect great things of you.
Open our eyes; astonish us with your goodness.
Make us ready for the good news of Jesus' coming. Amen.

Advent 3: A Story

The child John, born to Elizabeth and Zechariah in their old age, grew and became strong and was filled with the Holy Spirit. He had fine ancestors and grew up learning much from the priests and their families. He studied the Scriptures and understood that God expected him to be faithful. But John had a special job to do for God. John's mission was to be God's messenger and to announce the coming of Jesus, the Savior sent from God.

John knew that to be faithful to his mission, he had to show people there was a different way to live. He was different in so many ways. He left his comfortable home and went out into the wilderness where he ate insects and wild honey. He didn't cut his hair, he wore clothes made of camel skin, and he preached and preached and preached. Then he led people to the river to be baptized. John lived away from the things most people want because he believed something new was coming from God.

It wasn't hard for John to get people's attention. He was out there preaching and baptizing near the Jordan River where King Herod had built huge summer palaces with the money he'd taken from the people who kept getting poorer. John told those who came to hear him not to give up. He encouraged them to turn their lives toward God and have hope, because God would send Jesus, God's Son, to "defend the cause of the poor of the people, give deliverance to the needy, and crush the oppressor" *(Psalm 72:4)*. Jesus, the powerful One who was to follow John, would baptize, not just with water but with the Holy Spirit, and make possible a new life for everyone. Here are some of the words John spoke in his sermons, quoting the ancient prophet Isaiah:

A voice cries out:
"In the wilderness prepare the way of the Lord,
    make straight in the desert a highway for our God.
Every valley shall be lifted up,
    and every mountain and hill be made low;
the uneven ground shall become level,
    and the rough places a plain." *(Isaiah 40:3-5)*

God of wisdom and grace,
you sent John to prepare the people to receive your Son:
Make our hearts ready for the light of your presence
and the joy of your gift of Jesus Christ our Lord. Amen.

Advent 4: A Story

Elizabeth, John's mother, had a cousin named Mary, who was a very young woman engaged to marry a good man named Joseph. Not long after the angel appeared to Zechariah in the Temple, an angel appeared in Nazareth to Mary also. The angel said: "Greetings, favored one! The Lord is with you." Mary didn't know what to say or think, of course, so the angel continued, "Do not be afraid, Mary," . . . for you will "bear a son, and you will name him Jesus. He will be great, and will be called the Son of the Most High, and the Lord God will give to him the throne of his ancestor David, . . . and of his kingdom there will be no end" *(Luke 1:28-33)*.

Mary was still puzzled as to how she could become the mother of God's Son, so the angel told Mary that God had chosen her, and the Holy Spirit would come to her. To help Mary know about God's power, the angel said that Elizabeth, Mary's older cousin, was expecting a baby too, and this was a sign to Mary that "Nothing will be impossible with God" *(v. 37)* . Mary answered the angel's message from God with the best answer she could give: "Here am I, the servant of the Lord; let it be with me according to your word" *(v. 38)*. Soon Mary set out in a big hurry to travel to the hills of Judea to see Elizabeth for herself.

Elizabeth greeted Mary as soon as she walked in the house, and Elizabeth's baby, not yet born, seemed to know too that Mary was

God's favored one. Elizabeth was astounded that "the mother of our Lord" would visit her, and she felt the baby "leap for joy" at the sound of Mary's voice. She blessed Mary and praised her for her faith. The two women had so much to talk about and laugh about. They were happy and thankful, and Mary sang a joyful song of thanksgiving for God's goodness. Here is part of Mary's song:

My soul proclaims the greatness of the Lord,
my spirit rejoices in God my Savior. . . .
The arm of the Lord is strong,
    and has scattered the proud in their conceit.
God has cast down the mighty from their thrones,
    and lifted up the lowly.
God has filled the hungry with good things
    and sent the rich empty away.
God has come to the aid of Israel, the chosen servant
    remembering the promise of mercy,
    the promise made to our forebears,
    to Abraham and his children for ever.
(Luke 14:6-47, 51-55; ICET, rev. ELLC; from The United Methodist Hymnal, *199)*

**God of hope, we remember your mercy to us for generations:
Help us prepare for Jesus' coming by remembering those in need.
Give us grace, like Mary, to be the bearer of your love
and the instrument of your peace. In Jesus' name. Amen.**

Responsive Prayers for Small Groups, Households, and Church Programs

I. God of justice, you are patient with us
    and your patience is our salvation.

    Come and turn us toward your light.

    We want to be faithful people who turn to you.
    Restore us again, God of hope.

    Come and show us your grace.

    Renew your promise to bring peace to the earth
    and good will among all people, God of glory.

    Come and make us at home in your reign now.

    We wait for new heavens and a new earth.
    Speak peace to us, God of love.

    Come and teach us to strive for peace.

    Keep us in the embrace of love and faithfulness.
    Show us the place where peace and justice kiss.

    Come, Lord Jesus, surround us with your Spirit. Amen.

II. *L:* When the long night ends with the dawn's first rays,
    we want to be ready.

L: When the storm clouds break and the rainbow's light shines,
we want to be ready.
L: When valleys are high, hills are low, highways are straight,
we want to be ready.
L: When justice rolls down like the waters of a stream,
we want to be ready.
L: When the powerful are brought low and the lowly lifted up,
we want to be ready.
L: When the sick are healed and the hungry filled,
we want to be ready.
L: When all tears are wiped away and our joy is like the morning,
we want to be ready.
L: When God's glory is revealed, when Jesus our Savior comes,
we want to be ready.
L: God of hope, make us ready to celebrate the birth of Jesus, your Son and our Redeemer. Make us ready to live so that your reign of justice will touch all earth's people. Make us ready to welcome Jesus' coming again in glory and in light. With your Spirit's help, may we walk always in your light, through Jesus' name. Amen.
(first appeared in Homily Service, *December 1995; used by permission of The Liturgical Conference)*

III. Merciful God,
   you anointed Jesus to bring good news to the poor,
   bind up the broken hearted, declare release to the captives.
   comfort those who mourn, proclaim the Lord's favor:
   Hear our prayers for those in distress.

Come with us, God, that we may heal in your name.

We know you are a lover of justice:
Hear our prayers for those wait; give them hope.

Come with us, God, that we may find justice in your name.

We long for the day when your righteousness and praise
will spring up before the nations.
Hear our prayer for goodness and peace.

**Come with us, God, that we may be peacemakers in your
name.**

You have done great things for us;
prepare us to rejoice in the coming of your Son.
Hear our prayer for those who go out weeping.

**Come with us, God, that we may return to you with shouts of
joy. Amen.**

IV. Jesus, our Friend, you told all the children to come to you
and show us the way to live in your kingdom:
Come to us now and stay by our side.
Come, Lord Jesus.
Come, little children:
come to Bethlehem and see the manger.
Come, Lord Jesus.
Come, little children:
wait to see what's coming next.
Come, Lord Jesus.
We're waiting for Joseph;
we're waiting for Mary,
and a slow, old donkey.
Come, Lord Jesus.
We're waiting for a baby,
who brings us God's love.
Come, Lord Jesus.
We're waiting for the angels,
singing "Peace on earth."
Come, Lord Jesus.
We're waiting for the shepherds,
who heard the good news.
Come, Lord Jesus.

We're waiting for the magi,
who followed the star.
Come, Lord Jesus.
We're waiting for Jesus
to come to us now.
Come, Lord Jesus.
Come, little children:
come see what God has done.
Come and see the holy Child,
God's own true Son.
Come and sing glad songs
on this Christmas night
for God has sent us Jesus
with love and delight. Amen.

V. Jesus our Savior, remember with your mercy
those who are fed the bread of tears;
give courage and hope to those in danger.
Come to us and lead us like a flock.

Come, Lord Jesus. Restore us and let your face shine.

Put your hand on us and make us strong.
Show us your gift of life,
and we will call on your name.

Come, Lord Jesus. Restore us and let your face shine.

Release us from our fears.
Be near us through trouble and doubt;
grant us your peace.

Come, Lord Jesus. Restore us and let your face shine.

Keep us in life and death in your embrace.
Return to bring your glorious reign in all the world,
for you are the hope of the earth, joy of longing hearts.

Come, Lord Jesus. Restore us and let your face shine.

Make us ready to welcome you as the Prince of Peace,
the promised Emmanuel, the Sun of Righteousness.
Turn our eyes to the glorious power of your resurrection,
and open us to the grace you bring us all our days.

Come, Lord Jesus. Restore us and let your face shine. Amen.

PART TWO

Christmas

Introduction

"Lost in Wonder, Love, and Praise"

Christmas celebrations, even in our churches, come with their own set of difficulties. Our Puritan ancestors forbade them, the date has been the subject of numerous challenges, the Scrooges among us debunk the whole idea, and in our own time, Christmas has been captured by the market where it is known as the shopping season that will "make or break" many retail stores. But Christmas celebrations never fail to be observances of basic significance in our lives because they represent for us memory and hope; all year we recall "what we did last Christmas," and we begin to plan for "next Christmas" months ahead of time. The attention of most of us may be on the practicalities and details, but we know deep in our hearts that Christmas is a time to remember what God has done for us and to hope for the joyous feast when we will sit down with all the saints in glory.

The common complaint is that the Christmas season lasts too long, but historians of worship practices tell us that it is far too short. The unease with the length concerns the backing up of the shopping season to early fall, and the worry about the brevity, on the other hand, arises from the trend of sweeping Christmas out the door on December 26. At one time the church's season of Christmas, like Lent, lasted 40 days, from December 25 till February 2, the day of the feast that ends the season of light and hope: The Presentation of the Lord in the Temple or Candlemas. That wondrous feast is still celebrated, but now most church calendars mark the end of Christmas with the Baptism of the Lord on the first Sunday following January 6.

Christmas joy is lasting, and praise for the coming of Jesus should always remain part of our worship. In our attempt to take Christmas back from commercial interests, one thing we can do is to let our Christmas celebrations last at least through the Twelve Days. This suggestion may not be welcome to an exhausted church staff, but the resources in this book offer ideas for simpler celebrations and prayers that can be used in many situations. Some of the worship services can be led by lay people, and some are intended for use in the home, in church-related agencies, and with small groups.

The section called "The Twelve Days of Christmas," for example, can be used by households or individuals as devotional material. The stories and prayers also offer resources for planning daily prayer services in church groups and residential facilities. In addition, reading through the material for the Twelve Days can be of help to the congregation's worship planners as they work to find a sense of the season and meet the needs of a variety of worshipers. There are, in fact, resources for a baker's dozen, thirteen days, in this section because it begins with household prayers for Christmas Day.

The Twelve Days between December 25 and January 6 were once a significant time in the life of the church as days of preparation for adults who wished to be baptized at Epiphany. These special days still invite us to think about God's marvelous deeds and offer a time of preparation for renewed commitment to discipleship. There are several days of historical and biblical interest in this period that also suggest areas of pastoral concern. St. Stephen's Day, December 26, for example, is the day that the church chose to remember the first Christian martyr and is an appropriate day to remember the dying and those who grieve in this season of joy. In addition, the variety of liturgical observances on these days in churches around the world helps us remember our sisters and brothers who are still celebrating Christmas.

Standing on the Promises

The traditions are in place, the story is familiar, the songs will be sung. We don't really have to tell anyone how to celebrate Christmas, except that the world is not at peace, hungry children stare in sorrow from our TV screens, a friend is dying on Christmas Day, a family we know is breaking apart. How can we sing of Christmas joy when the shadow of death hangs over us?

We often say that Christmas is for children, and it is. Children enter into the Christmas story with abandon and bring adults along with them. Children learn from ritual and from celebrations, and we excel at both during the Christmas season. But Christmas is not only for children. There are parts of the Christmas story that are not even suitable for telling to children. The story is set in an atmosphere of political intrigue and treachery: Caesar is levying yet another tax on his conquered kingdoms; Herod is so afraid of the newborn King that he orders infants massacred. Our world is still beset by the greed of empires, some of them political and some corporate; and we react in horror and disbelief at what modern terrorists will do to children. So what has been changed by Jesus' birth?

The question is not a new one. Henry Wadsworth Longfellow put the situation of his own day this way in his poem "I Heard the Bells on Christmas Day": "For hate is strong and mocks the song / of peace on earth, good will to men." And answered himself: "God is not dead, nor doth he sleep. / The wrong shall fail; the right prevail." Edmund Sears, in the much-loved carol, "It Came upon the Midnight Clear," noted the misery of those who bear "life's crushing load" and offered them the encouragement of the ancient prophets: "Lo! the days are hastening on" when peace shall overtake the earth "and the whole world send back the song which now the angels sing." We cannot celebrate Christmas at all without standing on the promises of God.

We celebrate Christmas by standing on the promise that God's gift to us of Jesus Christ only begins in the manger. The story of Jesus' life on earth begins with his birth in a cave used as a stable and ends with his resurrection from a cave used as a tomb. Jesus left the manger behind and lived among us, full of grace and truth. We have witnesses to the events: The Gospels and Epistles tell us that he was born, lived, died, and was raised again to life. The shepherds saw him in the cave where he was born and the apostles saw the tomb, and ate and drank with the resurrected Jesus. We celebrate Christmas around an empty manger, an empty cross, and an empty tomb. That is good news, for "just as Christ was raised from the dead by the glory of the Father, so we too might walk in newness of life" *(Romans 6:4b).*

We celebrate Christmas by standing on the promise that God will hear our cries and stay near us. God will hear Rachel weeping for her children as God once heard the cries of the people held in slavery in Egypt and came down to deliver them from their suffering. What has changed in Jesus' birth is that Jesus became for us God made human, living among us, sharing all our suffering, even submitting to death on the cross. Jesus was willing to leave his throne and be born to a poor young woman who made his bed in a feeding trough. The infant Jesus lay there, as the German carol puts it, "naked and bare," exposed to all human afflictions, and yet "in him the fullness of God was pleased to dwell."

We celebrate Christmas by standing on the promise that Jesus will come again and that God will put all enemies, even death itself, under his footstool. "God will wipe every tear from their eyes. Death will be no more; mourning and crying and pain will be no more, for the first things have passed away" *(Revelation 12:4)*. The God who makes all things new will redeem us and all the earth with us by creating a new heaven and a new earth. We celebrate Christmas by remembering that God has already made us new creations in Jesus Christ. We celebrate Christmas by proclaiming that with the birth of Jesus God's reign of peace has already begun.

We are invited to observe Christmas with great joy. The Christmas feast we celebrate now is joyful because it is a foretaste of the heavenly feast, the banquet where God surrounds us with glory and joy forever. The wonder of Christmas calls us to pray again:

Finish, then, thy new creation; pure and spotless let us be.
Let us see thy great salvation perfectly restored in thee;
changed from glory into glory, till in heaven we take our place,
till we cast our crowns before thee, lost in wonder, love,
    and praise.
    (Charles Wesley, "Love Divine All Loves Excelling," 1747)

Christmas Eve

Christmas Eve, with its hectic activity and last-minute preparations, is far from a silent night in most twenty-first–century communities, but it is still a holy night. For this reason many congregations want to offer a variety of opportunities for people to gather in prayer at convenient hours. A candlelight Communion service or a service of lessons and carols is a grand tradition in many congregations. But there are times when something simpler is called for to meet the needs of a small congregation or of some members of a larger congregation who find a late evening or midnight service difficult to attend. An early evening, rather informal service is especially appropriate for families with young children, and the light of expectation on the children's faces is a treat for everyone.

The focal point of most family services is a nativity pageant with the cast made up entirely of children. Such a pageant has several advantages: The children make discoveries about the Christmas story from acting it out, and the congregation is blessed by the ministry of the children. In some way, having children as actors in a biblical presentation helps to preserve the mystery surrounding God's unfathomable love for the world, which is the heart of this drama, and also encourages the adults to suspend for a while their tendency to be critics and literalists. If the congregation is small, it may be necessary to include some adults in supporting roles, but whenever possible, children and youth should take the lead.

For an overworked church staff at Christmas, an elaborate production may be asking too much, but the pageant suggested below assumes minimal rehearsal time and simple costumes. The rehearsal is a good time for the children to talk about the story and ask questions, but if rehearsals are impossible to schedule, an improvised drama sometimes works well. The main requirement is a good leader who can give directions joyfully and can free people to use their imaginations. The leader provides a costume box from which "actors" pull out a prop or a piece of a costume that determines their role: ears made of cotton balls for a sheep, a crook for a shepherd, wings for an angel, a towel and ring of keys for the innkeeper. Even scenery can be improvised, or signs can be taped to designated areas, chairs, and screens, indicating "the inn," "the hillside," "the stable," and "the manger." Mary, Joseph, Gabriel, and a narrator and reader should be chosen in advance, receive some coaching, and perhaps have more definitive costumes.

Give children as many liturgical assignments in the celebration as possible. Older children can be readers and take up the offering. Include children in preparing Communion, carrying the bread and cup in procession to the table, and if allowed in your tradition, helping to serve. Ask a family or several families to make a special loaf of "Christmas bread" to serve at Communion. Talk about the service in classes and send home information sheets to parents. Joyous participation in worship is the way we thank God for the birth of Jesus and the way we become a part of the story of Christ's coming.

A Service of Prayer and Praise

Greeting

Tonight is a holy night: a night of stars and angels,
a night of shepherds and sheep, and a family in a stable.
Tonight we celebrate in memory and in hope
the birth of our Savior, the Holy Child of Bethlehem.

Thanks be to God.
Let all God's children come to the manger.

Hymn **"O Come, All Ye Faithful"**

Opening Prayer

Gather us around the manger, Lord Jesus;
let us sing in awe of the miracle of your birth.
You were born in the shadow of a cross,
and you came to be our Savior:
Give us grace to praise your gift of love,
to know the joy of the life you bring to all.
Give us the eyes of a child to see all things new
and the wisdom of a sage
to remember the promises of old.
Open our hearts to receive you joyfully,
for you are God's gift to the world,
in whose name we pray. **Amen.**

A Responsive Reading from Psalm 96

O sing to the Lord a new song;
sing, all the earth; bless God's holy name;
proclaim God's salvation from day to day.

Declare God's glory among the nations,
and sing God's marvelous works among all peoples.

For great is the Lord, and greatly to be praised.
No one is so great, neither kings nor other gods.

Honor and majesty are before the Lord;
strength and beauty are in God's sanctuary.

Honor the Lord, O families of the peoples,
Give thanks for God's glory and strength.
Worship the Lord in holy splendor;
Let all the earth tremble before our God.

Tell all the nations: "God is king!
The world has a firm foundation;
it shall never be moved.
God judges the peoples justly."

Let the heavens be glad, and let the earth rejoice;
let the sea roar and all that fills it;
let the fields shout and everything that grows.

Then shall all the trees of the forest sing for joy
before the Lord; for God is coming. *(based on Psalm 96)*

Hymn "Joy to the World"

The Christmas Story: A Nativity Pageant

(During the final stanza of the hymn, the narrator and reader go to the lectern. The narrator begins.)

Narrator:
A long time ago in a small, poor country, the emperor declared that all the world should be taxed. Everyone had to go to the place where their ancestors were born to register for the tax. That meant that Mary and Joseph had to go all the way from their home in Nazareth to Bethlehem, even though it was almost time for Mary's baby to be born.

(Mary and Joseph enter and walk slowly down the aisle during the reading and hymn.)

Reader: Luke 2:1, 3-5

Hymn "O Little Town of Bethlehem," stanza 1

Narrator:
They were tired when they reached Bethlehem, but all the rooms were already full. They knocked on the door of the inn, but the innkeeper said there was no room. Joseph told him that it was now time for Mary's baby to be born. The innkeeper took them to a place where there was a stable. The innkeeper said they could rest there. It was in the stable where the animals are kept that

Jesus was born. He had no cradle, so Mary laid him in the manger where hay was put out for the animals to eat.

(Mary, Joseph, and the innkeeper pantomime the actions during the next reading and hymn. When they reach the "stable," the "animals"—a cow, a donkey, a sheep, and possibly a lion and a lamb—join them around the manger.)

Reader: **Luke 2:6-7**

Hymn **"What Child Is This?" verses 1, 2**

Narrator:
On that same night some shepherds were on the hills near Bethlehem. Suddenly Gabriel and a whole host of heavenly angels appeared to them with a message from God: "Do not be afraid. Jesus the Savior is born."

(Light shifts to the "hillside" where shepherds and sheep are standing around. Gabriel appears, and the shepherds and sheep fall down. Gabriel says, "Do not be afraid. I bring you news of great joy. Jesus the Savior is born." The shepherds sit up. The "multitude" of angels appear and say in unison, "Glory to God in the highest, and peace to God's people on earth." They remain in place during the next reading and hymn.)

Reader: **Luke 2:8-14**

Hymn **"Angels We Have Heard on High," stanza 1**

Narrator:
The shepherds wasted no time. As soon as the angels left, the shepherds said to one another, "Let's go to Bethlehem and find the baby Jesus. Let's see this amazing thing that has happened."

(During the next reading, the shepherds leave the "hillside" and go quickly to the stable. They gather around the manger; those in front should kneel. The sheep can come too. As the last stanza of the hymn is sung, the angels may gather on either side of the stable.)

Reader: **Luke 2:15-16**

Hymn **"Away in a Manger," stanzas 1, 2, 3**

(The organist or pianist plays the song one more time for the actors to exit.)

Responsive Prayer of Thanksgiving

God of angels and shepherds,
we thank you for taking care of Mary and Joseph.
We thank you for the warm stable and the soft hay.
We thank you that Jesus your Son came to live on earth,
and that he was a sweet baby, cradled in his mother's arms.
Help us remember that he sometimes cried and got hungry.
Help us remember that he was like us in every way,
but he was also your holy Son.

**Glory to God in the highest,
and peace to God's people on earth.**

God of all the earth's people,
we thank you that Jesus grew and became strong.
We thank you that he welcomed children and blessed them.
We thank you that he taught the people who came to him,
and that he healed the sick and fed those who were hungry.
Help us to remember that he loved us enough to die for us.
Help us to remember that you raised him to life again
and that he is our friend and reigns with you forever.

**Glory to God in the highest,
and peace to God's people on earth.**

God of glory,
we thank you for Christmas, for laughter and singing,
for family and friends, for presents and good food.
Help us to remember the people who are hungry,
the people who are sick or sad, the people who are afraid.
Help us to remember all year long that Jesus is the Prince of peace.

**Glory to God in the highest
and peace to God's people on earth.**

In Jesus' name. Amen.

Response to Prayer "O Little Town of Bethlehem," stanza 4

Offering

> *(A carol is offered by an instrumentalist, a choir, or a soloist)*

Prayer after the Offering

> We present these gifts to you, O God,
> and ask that you accept them
> for the work of your reign of peace.
> On this night of marvelous gifts
> we ask, "What more can I give to Jesus?"
> Help us to bring ourselves to Jesus with great joy.
> For the gift of Jesus and for all your blessings,
> we give you thanks and praise. **Amen.**

Hymn **"Good Christian Friends, Rejoice"**

The Lord's Supper (Please use the Communion liturgy from your denominational worship book.)

Unison Prayer of Thanksgiving after Communion
> **We thank you, God, for this holy place,**
> **for bringing us together at your table,**
> **surrounded by your love.**
> **We thank you for this holy meal,**
> **for inviting us to accept Jesus' gift of himself,**
> **for asking us to taste and see how much Jesus loves us.**
> **We thank you for this holy night,**
> **for the glad songs we sing**
> **and the gifts of love we receive.**
> **Help us to give ourselves in love and joy.**
> **In the name of Jesus our Savior. Amen.**

Hymn **"Silent Night"**

Blessing and Dismissal

> The heralds on the mountains bring us good news of great joy: Jesus Christ has come to preach peace in all the world. Go and tell everyone you meet all that you have seen and heard. The grace of

our Lord Jesus Christ, the love of God, and the communion of the Holy Spirit go with us all. **Amen.**

The peace of Christ be with you.
And also with you.

(The people may greet one another in the name of Christ.)

Prayers for Christmas Day and the Sundays of Christmas

Christmas Day

Greeting

The heralds of peace are on the mountains,
bringing good news: God reigns!
All the ends of the earth shall see God's glory.
Let us lift up our voices and break into singing:
"Joy to the world, the Lord is come."

Call to Worship

O sing to the LORD a new song.

The LORD has done marvelous things.

Let the sea roar, and all that fills it;
the world and those who live in it.

**Let the hills sing together for joy,
for the LORD is with us.
Make a joyful noise.
Thanks be to God.** *(based on Psalm 98)*

Opening Prayer

God of earth and heaven:
when you brought your firstborn into the world,
you sent your angel messengers, swift as the winds,
and your servants, like flames of fire, to tell the glad news:
Give us courage in the midst of all earth's shadows
to praise you for the Light that overcomes;
to sing the glory of your beloved Son,
who came to live among us, full of grace and truth.
In his name we pray. **Amen.**

Call to Confession

"No more let sins and sorrows grow." Jesus calls us to live in his
light, to "prove the glories of his righteousness, and wonders of
his love." Let us turn to God for forgiveness and life.
(quotations from Isaac Watts, "Joy to the World," stanza 3)

Prayer of Confession

God of glory, you sent your Son to take away our sins:
We celebrate Jesus' birth, and we ask you to change us,
heal us, make us your children.
Help us to praise you by our lives for the gift of Jesus.
Keep us from neglecting to honor Jesus with gifts of mercy and
kindness,
from failing to welcome your perfect love with love for each
other,
from allowing lesser lights to blind us to the Light that over-
comes,
from forgetting the call of the needy and the cry of the world
for peace.
We give you thanks for the love of Jesus, our friend,
who lives among us. Amen.

Words of Assurance

Good Christian friends, rejoice!
Jesus Christ was born to save.
He has opened heaven's door,

and we are blessed forever more.
Christ was born for this!
Christ was born for this!
("Good Christian Friends, Rejoice," 14th-century Latin, from stanzas 3, 4)

Acts of Praise A Reading from Luke's Gospel with Carols

Reader:	Hear the good news according to Luke.
	Luke 2:1-7
Congregation:	**"Once in Royal David's City"**
Reader:	**Luke 2:8-14**
Congregation:	**"It Came upon the Midnight Clear"**
Reader:	**Luke 2:15-16**
Congregation:	**"Infant Holy, Infant Lowly"**
Reader:	**Luke 2:17-20**
Congregation:	**"Go, Tell It on the Mountain"**

Prayer for Illumination

Steadfast and ever loving God,
you anointed Jesus with the oil of gladness
and brought him into the world
to reflect your glory:
Give us joyful hearts
that we may welcome the Word of life
and come to know you
through the Light that cannot be overcome.
In Jesus' name. **Amen.**

Prayer of Thanksgiving after the Offering

Mighty God, you founded the earth;
the heavens are the work of your hands:

We bring to you gifts of your own making;
we honor you with what you have given us.
We thank you for the goodness of this day
   and the bounty we enjoy.
Accept our praise for the gift of Jesus Christ,
   in whose name we pray. Amen.

Prayers of Intercession and Thanksgiving

God of all creation,
your angels sang a new song on the mountains,
a song of good news to all the earth:
Lift up our eyes to the singing hills;
open our ears to the roaring sea, the clapping rivers;
open our hearts to those around us,
that we may praise you with our whole lives
and know the joy of your presence.
For the coming of your Word to live among us,

we give you grateful thanks.

We praise you for the victory that is yours, O God,
for the gift of your Son who laid down his glory
and was born in a stable to share our weakness
   and die our death that we may one day live with him.
We thank you for Christ's rising,
   for the healing in his wings,
   and for the light and life he brings to all.
For the coming of the Light that cannot be overcome,

we give you grateful thanks.

Give us grace to be with those in sorrow this day,
   to weep with those who cannot sing for joy.
Grant your peace to the sick, the grieving, the dying;
comfort them with your presence.
Give us grateful hearts for Christmas feasts
   and loved ones gathered round our tables.
Show us the way to share our food and love
   with hungry people everywhere,

and bring us all to your great banquet feast of joy.
For the coming of your Son,
who gives us power to become your children,

we give you grateful thanks.

We thank you for the life Christ's coming brings.
Grant us grace to know him as one of us,
and walk with him in newness of life all our days.
Through Jesus Christ, Holy Child and Savior. **Amen.**

Commission and Blessing

Gloria in excelsis Deo!
Glory to God in the highest
and peace to God's people on earth.
Praise God for all we have seen and heard.
Go in peace and tell everyone you meet:
Christ is born! Do not be afraid.
Thanks be to God!

First Sunday After Christmas Day

Greeting

Our own eyes have seen the salvation God prepared
for all peoples,
a light for revelation to the Gentiles
and glory to God's people Israel.
Thanks be to God!   *(based on Luke 2:30-32)*

Call to Worship

God has clothed us with garments of salvation
and adorned us with garlands like a bride and groom.

We will greatly rejoice in the Lord;
we will praise God with our whole being.

God the gardener has planted the seed and watered it.
God will cause the shoot to spring up.

God will bring forth goodness and praise before all nations.
The LORD gives us a new name and crowns us with beauty.
(based on Isaiah 61:10–62:3)

Opening Prayer

Gracious God, in the fullness of time,
you sent your Son, born of a woman,
so that we might receive adoption as children,
   and we give you thanks.
Bind us together in perfect harmony.
Give us grace to clothe ourselves in love,
to make a home for Christ's word in us,
and to do everything in the name of the Lord Jesus.
In his name we pray. **Amen.**
(based on Galatians 4:4-5; Colossians 3:12-17)

Call to Confession

Christ our brother became like us in every respect, and because he
was tested by what he suffered, he is able to help us when we are
tested *(based on Hebrews 2:17-18).* Let us go to God in prayer
and ask for Christ's promised help in living holy and acceptable
lives.

Prayer of Confession

God of love, in gratitude for your gracious deeds,
we look to the coming new year for renewal.
You have made us your children;
now we ask for your help in turning our lives toward you.
   Make us thankful people, praising you in all we do.
   Free us to sing with joy the psalms and hymns of praise.
   Teach us to forgive others as Christ forgives us.
   Show us the way of compassion, kindness, and patience.

Give us grace to let the peace of Christ live in our hearts.
We pray in the name of our Lord Jesus Christ. Amen.

(based on Colossians 3:12-17)

Words of Assurance

Christ is a merciful and faithful high priest in the service of God. Through his death and resurrection, Christ has freed our lives and forgiven us *(based on Hebrews 2:14, 17)*. Thanks be to God.

Acts of Praise **Celebrating God's Creation: Psalm 148**

As an act of praise, ask the children's choir or a children's church school class to prepare ahead of time and act out Psalm 148. Puppets or costumes—angels, sun, stars, snowflakes, animals, for example—may be used. The children may lead the congregation in singing an appropriate song or hymn and in the responsive reading of the psalm from the hymnal or the adapted version below.

Praise the Lord! Praise the Lord from the heavens:
angels and all the heavenly host, sun, moon, and stars.

Praise the Lord! Praise the Lord from the earth:
mountains and hills, fruit trees and evergreens,
wild animals and cattle, creeping things and flying birds,
sea creatures, fire, hail, snow, frost, and stormy wind.

Praise the Lord, who spoke and you were created,
who established you forever and set your boundaries.

Praise the Lord, all rulers of the earth and all peoples,
young men and women alike, old and young together!
Let all God's faithful people praise the Lord!

(based on Psalm 148)

Hymn Suggestion: "All Things Bright and Beautiful"

(first appeared in Blair Gilmer Meeks, Season of Ash and Fire *[Nashville: Abingdon Press, 2004], 80)*

99

Prayer for Illumination

God of light, you shine on us like the dawn:
Show us again the salvation you have sent,
and make us your thankful people.
Send the Spirit of your Son into our hearts,
and show us how to learn from you
as children learn from parents.
Give us grace to teach one another with gratitude,
doing all things in the name of the Lord Jesus. **Amen.**

Prayer of Thanksgiving after the Offering

We come before you, O Lord,
rejoicing in the abundance of your steadfast love.
Your acts of grace are more than we can count;
we treasure them in our hearts.
In joy and praise, we return to you these gifts.
In the name of Jesus Christ. **Amen.**

Prayers of Intercession and Thanksgiving

God of hope, you are the One who makes all things new.
We give you thanks for the beginning of a new year.
We praise you for the newness we have through Jesus Christ.
Free us from our fears; lift us up from our doubts
and help us enter into the new thing you are doing.
Walk with us through all our days, O Lord,

and we will put our trust in you.

We lay before you the troubles of the world:
the constant threat of terror, the pervasiveness of violence,
the affliction of hunger and disease, the menace of greed,
the deaths of children who had no chance at life.
We call to you in our distress, for you are also distressed;
you are the One who redeems us in love and pity.
Save us with your presence; lead us on the path to peace.
Walk with us through all our days, O Lord,

and we will put our trust in you.

We thank you for celebrations held throughout the world,
for sisters and brothers who sing with us songs of Jesus' birth.
Give us unity in your love; send us the Spirit of Christ.
Help us to grow and become strong;
fill us with wisdom and the favor of God.
Bring us to your table, amazed by your grace,
and make us ready to enter your new creation.
Walk with us through all our days, O Lord,

and we will put our trust in you.
In Jesus' name. Amen.

Commission and Blessing

God will dismiss us now in peace,
as God dismissed Simeon,
    who held and blessed God's holy Son.
God will give us grace, like the grace of Anna,
that we may go and speak with joy
concerning the child Jesus,
    given by God to be our peace.
Give God thanks and praise.

Thanks be to God.

Epiphany Sunday

Greeting

Arise, shine; for your light has come,
and the glory of the LORD has risen upon you. *(Isaiah 60:1)*
Come all who have seen the light of the star.
Come and seek the Prince of Peace, the hope of all the earth.

Call to Worship

Lift up your eyes and look around.
Gather from East and West, North and South.

Our sons and daughters are coming from far away.
Camels will come bearing gifts of gold and frankincense.

Nations will come and bring abundant gifts.
Sovereigns will come to see the dawn of God's reign.

We will see the light rising upon us and be radiant.
We will rejoice and proclaim the praise of the Lord.
                                    (based on Isaiah 60:4-6)

Opening Prayer

God of grace, we have seen the rising of your light
and we will follow it with joy:
Lead us to the One who rules in love.
Guide us to the place where peace abounds.
Show us the way to your justice and mercy.
Direct our journeys to the birthplace of your truth.
In the name of Jesus Christ, the beginning and the end. **Amen.**

Call to Confession

God's great gift of love was greeted by shepherds and sages, coming from rough places and foreign lands. Earth's people are drawn
to the birthplace of God's chosen One, sent to a weary world to
wash away our sins. Let us pray to God for forgiveness and mercy.

Prayer of Confession

God of love,
you watch in sorrow as nation rises up against nation,
    as brothers and sisters live in strife.
Forgive us for tolerating injustice.
Forgive us for the fear that leads to hate.
Forgive us when we fail to lead the way to peace.
Guide us by your light to the dawn of Christ's reign of peace,

where strangers bearing gifts meet to worship Christ our Lord. In Christ's name we pray. Amen.

Words of Assurance

God's mercy falls on us like rain on the mown grass, like showers that water the earth. Thanks be to God.

Acts of Praise **Gifts for a Baby Born to Be King**

A storyteller gathers the children in the congregation for a story and has come prepared with gifts to give the children after the story. The gifts are birthday candles, triangles of pita bread wrapped in napkins, and small pieces of wood that can be formed into crosses.

A long time ago, some very wise people who lived in Persia saw a great light in the sky. They were professors, and it was their job to study the stars and planets and give advice to the king. They knew this was no ordinary star, and they searched their books and scratched their heads. None of them had a clue about where the star could have come from. What was even more puzzling, the star seemed to move in the night sky. They thought there must be a reason for this blazing heavenly object, and they knew that the only way to discover what it meant was to begin a quest. On most occasions when they had seen a new star above, a prince or princess had been born, or a great hero. Curious about the new bright star that moved in a strange direction, they went off on a long, long journey in search of a baby, born to be a king.

They traveled for weeks over hot deserts and rugged mountains, through forests full of wild animals, and on lonely roads where there were robbers. The star led them every step of the way. At last they came to Jerusalem, the capital city of a small country they had barely even heard of. They found the palace of the king—his name was King Herod—and presented him with letters of introduction from their own king. They told him they were looking for a baby, born to be king. This was an unpleasant surprise to King Herod, who expected his own son to be crowned one day. But one of the king's advisors at court knew of an ancient prophecy that said God would send the people a just ruler, descended from King David, who would be born in Bethlehem.

Bethlehem was a poor village in the hills some distance up the road, and so the wise travelers from Persia took off immediately, still following the star. At last the star stopped moving and so did they. The light of the star shone over a small house in the town of Bethlehem. Now everyone knows you don't go to visit a new baby without gifts, so the Persian professors—some people call them sages or magi—unpacked their gifts and went in the house. There they found Mary, Joseph, and Jesus, a beautiful child whose face shone with the light of God. They knew they had found the right place, and they were overwhelmed with joy. The travelers from Persia knelt before the baby, who was God's chosen One, sent to rule over the world in peace.

The gifts they brought—gold, frankincense, and myrrh—were expensive; they were fit for a king. The gifts also meant something, as all good gifts do. They showed that the wise men knew that baby Jesus was royalty, a baby born to be king. The gifts showed that Jesus was more than an ordinary king; they showed that he was sent from God. Finally, the gifts showed that the wise men knew how much Jesus loves us and that he came to bring us the gift of his life.

I have some gifts for you today. They aren't expensive gifts like the ones the rich magi of Persia brought to baby Jesus, but they will help you remember that Jesus loves you.

First, I have a candle, to remind you that Jesus said, "I am the light of the world." Jesus is the light sent from God to shine away all our fears. *(Hold up a candle.)*

Next, I have a piece of bread because Jesus also said, "I am the bread of life." Jesus wants to feed all the people of the world, so that no one is hungry any more. *(Hold up a piece of bread.)*

And I have two pieces of wood. Jesus grew up in a carpenter shop and played with scraps of wood as a child. When he was grown, he gave his life for us and died on a cross, which is made from two pieces of wood like this. *(Demonstrate by holding the wood in the shape of a cross.)* God raised Jesus to life again and gave him the power to rule over all. Jesus was born to be God's chosen king. He is also our friend. That's how much Jesus loves us.

Hymn Suggestions: "De Tierra Lejana Venimos (From a Distant Home)"; "Angels from the Realms of Glory"

(Sung as the children receive their gifts and go to their seats or classrooms.)

Prayer for Illumination

Reveal to us, O God, the mystery of Christ,
disclosed by the Spirit to the apostles and prophets.
Empower your church to make known
the wisdom of God in all its richness
that we may live in accordance with the eternal purpose,
carried out through Christ Jesus our Lord,
in whose name we pray. **Amen.** *(based on Ephesians 3:1-12)*

Prayer of Thanksgiving after the Offering

Gracious God, we thank you for all good gifts.
   You have shown us how to give with love:
   Accept the gifts we bring;
use them for the work of Jesus' reign.
Keep us in remembrance of the magi
and grant us their generosity and courage.
In the name of Jesus, your greatest gift. **Amen.**

Prayers of Intercession and Thanksgiving

God of all our comings and goings,
we give you grateful thanks
   for your light that guides us on our way,
   for your tender care that holds us close,
   for your strong, protecting arm.
Keep us on the right path and safe from harm.
Lord, in your mercy,

hear our prayer.

In your graciousness, you have sent your Son,
   the promised Ruler who will judge with mercy
   and defend the cause of the poor.

Open our hearts to the call of the needy.
Give us grace to help those who have no helper.
Give us courage to stand against oppression and tyranny.
Give us compassion for those who suffer.
Lord, in your mercy,

hear our prayer.

As you protected Joseph, Mary, and Jesus
    and sent them to safety in Egypt,
    protect all who travel far from home.
Keep in your care the men and women stationed abroad,
    and comfort the families they leave behind.
Go with the students who leave to return to their studies.
Make your presence known to all who travel in their work.
Remember the homeless in our communities.
Help the refugees from famine and oppression
    and all who flee from violence.
Lord, in your mercy,

hear our prayer.

We give you thanks for all who have come before us:
    for the prophets and apostles, the faithful disciples,
    the women and men who saw your light
    and received the news of the boundless riches of Jesus Christ.
We thank you for the church that makes known to us
    the rich variety of your wisdom and your eternal purpose.
We give you praise and thanks for Jesus Christ our Lord,
    and for our faith in him that brings us boldly into your presence.
In Jesus' name we pray. **Amen.**

Commission and Blessing

We rejoice this day in the rising of the Sun of righteousness, the coming of the heaven-born Prince of Peace. Let us go out in love, ready to spread the news of the light and life he brings to all the earth. The peace of Christ go with you.

And also with you.

Baptism of the Lord

Greeting

But now thus says the LORD, the One who created you:
Do not fear, for I have redeemed you;
I have called you by name, you are mine. *(based on Isaiah 43:1)*
The Lord be with you.

And also with you.

Call to Worship

Let all who serve the LORD give God glory;
Let all creation honor God's glory and strength.

**Honor God's glorious name;
worship the LORD in holy splendor.**

The voice of the LORD thunders over the waters;
God's voice is powerful and full of majesty.

**The LORD rules over all:
May the LORD give strength to the people.
May God bless the people with peace.**
                    (based on Psalm 29:1-4, 10-11)

Opening Prayer

God of power and might,
you call the wind to whirl the oaks;
your voice flashes flames of fire:
Send your Spirit to anoint us for your work.
Renew in us your covenant of love;
give us thankful hearts in remembrance of our baptism.
Through Jesus Christ our Lord. **Amen.**

Call to Confession

God, who has written the covenant on our hearts, will forgive us and remember our sins no more. Let us ask God to forgive our sins and cleanse us.

Prayer of Confession

God of mercy,
We thank you for the gift of baptism by water and the Spirit.
Keep us mindful of the promises we have made
  to renounce the forces of evil in the world
  and forsake the ways of sin that alienate us from you.
Help us to resist evil, injustice, and oppression in all forms.
Give us grace to call Jesus Christ our Savior
  and serve him as our Lord.
We acknowledge that we have not always been diligent,
  that we at times fail to represent Christ in the world
  and to support his church in unity and praise.
Forgive and cleanse us;
Make us faithful members of Christ's body.
In the name of Christ, your beloved Son. Amen.

Words of Assurance

"John announced after the baptism how God anointed Jesus of Nazareth with the Holy Spirit and with power. . . . All the prophets testify about him that everyone who believes in him receives forgiveness of sins through his name." *(Acts 1:37-38, 43)* Thanks be to God.

Acts of Praise
Called to New Life from the Waters of Baptism:
A Responsive Reading

At the creation God's Spirit swept over the surface of the waters.
God divided the waters into sky and sea and created the dry land.
God called forth light and brought life from the face of the deep.
(See Genesis 1:1-15.)

God our creator makes all things new:
Give God thanks and praise.

God brought Noah, his family, and all kinds of creatures through the waters of the flood to live in faithfulness and peace. The bow in the clouds is the sign of the covenant of peace that God has made with the earth and every living being. *(See Genesis 9:12-17.)*

God's steadfast love endures forever:
Give God thanks and praise.

By a strong east wind, the Lord drove back the waters of the sea, and the Hebrew slaves of Pharaoh crossed the sea on dry land. God's awesome might brings God's people through the waters to a new life of freedom. *(See Exodus 14:21-22.)*

God has given us a marvelous victory:
Give God thanks and praise.

John baptized Jesus in the waters of the Jordan. When Jesus came up from the river, he saw the Spirit of God descending like a dove and heard a voice from heaven saying, "This is my Son, the Beloved." *(See Matthew 3:13-17.)*

God sends Jesus, the anointed One, to preach peace:
Give God thanks and praise.

In the waters of baptism we are buried with Christ, and as Christ was raised from the dead, so we will rise with Christ and walk with him in newness of life. *(See Romans 6:4.)*

By Jesus' death and resurrection we are given life:
Give God thanks and praise.

Prayer for Illumination

God our help and hope,
you created us for your glory:
Give us your word within our hearts
that we may know you.
Take us by the hand and lead us;
bring our sons and daughters from far away
and make us your people.
In Jesus' name. **Amen.**

Prayer of Thanksgiving after the Offering

We come with thanksgiving to bring you our gifts, O God.
We thank you for the spiritual gifts received at our baptism
and for the gift of Jesus Christ, the joy of heaven,
who came to earth and was anointed by your Spirit.
We praise you for raising him up to reign with you
and the Holy Spirit, now and forever. **Amen.**

Prayers of Intercession and Thanksgiving

God of life,
in baptism you give us forgiveness and new life,
anointing us with your Holy Spirit
and making us members of Christ's body:
Keep us faithful in your covenant;
embrace us with your love.
You have called us through water and the Spirit:

Help us to live as faithful disciples of Jesus Christ.

You have given us the Spirit of justice and compassion:
Lead us to respond with works of mercy and kindness.
Teach us to care for your children and know their names:
those whose lives bring joy to all around them
and those who are hungry and neglected.
Give us the courage of Jesus' caring presence,
that we may faithfully visit the sick and those in prison.
Keep us in mind of Jesus' forgiveness of others,
that we may forgive those who sin against us.
Guide us to accept all who love you without partiality,
that we may welcome strangers in communion with you.
You have called us through water and the Spirit:

Help us to live as faithful disciples of Jesus Christ.

You have called us by name and redeemed us;
now with thanksgiving we hear you call us your beloved.
Make us strong so that your church may be strong.
Keep us in remembrance of our baptism
that we may live joyful, useful lives in thanksgiving to you.

Bring us at last to the river that flows from your throne,
where you reign with Jesus Christ and the Holy Spirit,
   now and forever. **Amen.**

Commission and Blessing

God calls us to follow Jesus in bringing sight to those without
understanding, freedom to those imprisoned by sin and fear of
death, and light to the all nations. *(Isaiah 42:6-7)*

God promises to bless us with peace.
The peace of Christ be with you.

And also with you.

New Year's Eve or Day

At New Year's our thoughts are filled with memories of times past and hopes for the coming year. For many congregations these thoughts are gathered around covenant renewal, either at a service of baptismal reaffirmation in remembrance of Christ's baptism or at a traditional Wesleyan Covenant Service. Celebrations for the Reaffirmation of Baptismal Vows are found in most newer denominational books of worship, and the Covenant Service in several forms is in Methodist worship books from many countries. For a complete Covenant Service based on John Wesley's writings and his Covenant Prayer, see *The New Handbook of the Christian Year* (Hoyt L. Hickman, et al., Nashville: Abingdon Press, 1992).

The order of worship that follows here will help congregations prepare for beginning the new year with renewed commitment to discipleship and a covenant relationship with God. It can stand on its own or be used as a preparation for a covenant service or baptismal renewal on another day. The service is appropriate for ecumenical use, with the eventuality that in some settings, it may be necessary to omit the serving of Communion. The readings will remind us of God's covenant-making with God's people, and there will be time for remembering God's blessings and for accepting our calling to be disciples of Jesus Christ in silent and corporate prayer. The scripture readings should be given by experienced readers who have rehearsed, and the hymns following the scriptures can be sung by congregation, choir, or soloists.

A Service for the New Year

Remembering God's Covenant

Greeting

Hear the words of the prophet Isaiah:
"I am the LORD, that is my name;
    my glory I give to no other, . . .
See, the former things have come to pass,
and new things I now declare;
before they spring forth,
I tell you of them." *(Isaiah 42:8-9)*

Friends, we have come together to remember God's gracious acts
to us and our ancestors in the faith and to give thanks for the new
things God has promised to do among us.

Call to Worship

LORD, you have been our dwelling place in all generations.

**Before the mountains were brought forth,
or ever you had formed the earth,
from everlasting to everlasting you are God.**

Satisfy us in the morning with your steadfast love
so that we may rejoice and be glad all out days.

**Let the favor of the Lord our God be upon us
and prosper for us the work of our hands—
O prosper the work of our hands!**
    (based on Psalm 90)

Hymn **"Love Divine, All Loves Excelling"**

Opening Prayer

Mighty God, you have done great things:
You have made us a new creation in Jesus Christ,
   and you send us your Spirit to guide us on the way:
Turn us away from worries and distractions,
that we may see you clearly
and bring your light to all who live in the shadows.
In Jesus' name. **Amen.**

The Ministry of the Word

*(A leader and four readers come forward. Each carries a white pil-
lar candle, which will be lighted by an acolyte and then placed by
the reader on a central table as each reading begins. The leader's
candle is lighted preceding the reading of the psalm.)*

Leader:
Let us open God's word and hear again the accounts of God's
marvelous deeds. May God give us grace to accept these words as
an invitation to draw closer to God and commit ourselves in
service to Christ.

Reader: **A reading from the Law: Deuteronomy 29:10-15**

Hymn **"The God of Abraham Praise"**

Reader: **A reading from the Prophets: Jeremiah 31:31-34**

Hymn **"Great Is Thy Faithfulness"**

Leader: Let us read together Psalm 19 responsively. **Psalm 19**

Hymn **"I Sing the (Al)Mighty Power of God"**

Reader: **A reading from the Epistles: Romans 12:1-2**

Hymn **"Take My Life and Let It Be"**

Reader: **A reading from the Gospel according to John: John 15:1-10**

Hymn "**Help Us Accept Each Other**"

The Ministry of Prayer

Silent Prayer

> *Leader:*
> Let us enter into a time of silence. In the quiet of this place, let us prepare our hearts and minds to serve God in the coming year and be ready to listen for God's still, small voice in our lives.
>
> *(A chorus may be sung: "Lord, Prepare Me to Be a Sanctuary," for example.)*
>
> *Silence is kept.*

Prayers of Thanksgiving and Intercession

> *Leader:*
> Let us join now in offering our common thanksgivings and petitions to God, remembering our concern for the church, our nation and all nations, and all persons in need. Please respond to the words "Lord, in your mercy," saying "hear our prayer." Let us pray.
>
> Holy God, you are high and lifted up, your garments fill the Temple, and yet you are very near to us: We thank you for your glorious presence that calls us to a holy life, for your Son who left his throne and became obedient to the cross so that we might have life, and for the gift of your Spirit who brings us your peace. Cleanse us and make us whole.
>
> Lord, in your mercy,
>
> **hear our prayer.**
>
> *Leader:*
> Strengthen the church in its witness to the world. Guide pastors, officials, and lay persons; encourage us in our ministry; keep us true to your word. Give us compassion and understanding so that by the power of your Spirit, we may embrace each other in unity, one body through all the earth.
>
> Lord, in your mercy,

hear our prayer.

Leader:
Give courage and discretion to the rulers of nations that they may stand up against oppression and greed and put an end to cycles of violence and hate. Remember all who serve their country in dangerous places. Keep safe the aid and health workers who bring food and healing to suffering people. Guide negotiators and all who work to bring truth and reconciliation in places of conflict.

Lord, in your mercy,

hear our prayer.

Leader:
Help us to remember your children everywhere, the joy of those who sing your praise, the cries of those who are never filled. Teach us their names and guide us to be their protectors and advocates. Show us how to bring them your care: to heal the sick, to give shelter to the homeless, and to embrace the orphans.

Lord, in your mercy,

hear our prayer.

Leader:
Hold in your care those who grieve. Share the sorrow of those who mourn for their countries, torn by war or devastated by famine, disaster, and disease. Weep with those whose hearts ache with emptiness at the death of a loved one. Show them the mercy of your love, for you sent your Son that through our baptism we might die with him and live again in the promise of being raised like him to life in your glorious home.

Lord, in your mercy,

hear our prayer.

Leader:
We give you thanks and praise for the beginning of a new year, for the freedom we enjoy as your sons and daughters, and for the newness we have through Jesus Christ. Free us from our fears and

doubts, and help us enter into the new thing you are doing among us. Give us grace to live our lives every day in service to Jesus Christ our Lord. In his name we pray. **Amen.**

The Lord's Supper

Hymn **"I Come with Joy"**

The Thanksgiving

The Lord's Prayer

The Breaking of the Bread

Prayers and Dismissal

Let us pray together.

**Faithful God,
with these holy gifts
you have fed and strengthened us
in Jesus Christ your Son.
Guide us on our way,
that with all your faithful people
we may come to share the feast
of your eternal kingdom;
through Jesus Christ our Lord. Amen.**

Hymn **"Now Thank We All Our God"**

Blessing

The grace of our Lord Jesus Christ,
the love of God, and the communion of the Holy Spirit,
be with us all. **Amen.**

The Lord has made an everlasting covenant of peace with God's people.

The peace of the Lord be with you.

And also with you.

(The people may greet one another in the name of Christ.)

A Celebration for the Day of Epiphany

Epiphany is most often celebrated in our churches on the Sunday that falls on or before January 6. There are, however, situations where a weekday observance is possible and desirable. Among those possibilities are regularly scheduled Wednesday night programs, ecumenical Twelfth-Night celebrations among several neighborhood churches, and celebrations in church-related institutions—agency offices, residential healthcare centers, schools, or colleges. What follows are suggestions for weekday celebrations and an order of worship that can be adapted for any of these uses as well as for family gatherings and small group meetings.

The popular notion of a nativity scene is that of shepherds and sheep, magi and camels all jumbled up together around the manger; and for the dramatic purposes of a children's pageant, we are happy, of course, to leave this collage alone. To be faithful to the accounts of Matthew and Luke, however, we recognize that each Gospel has its own story; each has a significant theological perspective that may not be fully grasped when the stories are joined. For this reason, the church calendar offers us the opportunity to celebrate both stories fully in separate observances. On December 25, Luke's narrative of the shepherds' hearing the angels and arriving at the manger is read; and on January 6, Epiphany, Matthew's account of the journey of the magi is the focus. Each celebration also has a unique set of symbols. God's great act of love is held in our minds and hearts through the rich and varied images the Gospel writers have laid out for us.

Most of us have memories associated with Epiphany that include brilliant colors, imaginative costumes, and deep male voices singing about the "kings'" gifts. The problem with these memories is that they sometimes engender unrealistic expectations: expensive costumes and operatic baritones are beyond the reach of many congregations. In addition, some of our ideas about what happened—that the visitors were kings and that there were three of them, for example—are conjecture not Gospel and need not determine our planning. All planners should begin by studying, with the help of commentaries and other resources, the story in Matthew 2, including the context of Herod's actions. This time of study will help keep the focus on what is important.

An Epiphany procession is important. It is, in fact, the focal point, a dramatic way of telling the story, an act of worship that will be long remembered and therefore should be carefully planned and rehearsed. This is first of all a worship service that includes a grand liturgical procession, and the processors should be not only the magi but also a starbearer, the acolytes, a Bible bearer, a cross bearer, the preacher or storyteller, readers, musicians—anyone who has a liturgical role. The congregation sings, and the gifts are brought forward, the magi's gifts but also the gifts of the people. In preparation for this service the planning committee can designate an offering for outreach and ask people to bring gifts to the celebration: canned food, clothing and toys, cards pledging mission or service commitments, for example. The offerings are collected at the door to be carried in the procession and placed with the magi's gifts. One focus of Matthew's story is the coming of Christ to the whole world, and to emphasize this, those who bring forward the offering—children or adults—may dress in traditional ethnic or national clothing. Following the placing of the gifts, the gift bearers can surround or face the congregation and remain in place through the psalm.

Costumes for the magi are effective, but they needn't be opulent. The magi were weary travelers and probably not kings but scholars who specialized in understanding the stars. They also represent the "foreigners" at Jesus' birth, so they may wear clothing that suggests the wide world that their legends say they represent: We often imagine them to be of European, Asian, and African origins. The sages may also be accompanied by banner bearers, drummers, bell ringers, and pages if space allows. The usual practice is for the magi to process around the room several times before arriving at "Bethlehem," where the starbearer—who carries a single star mounted on the end of a pole, or a banner with a large star in the center—leads them and stops. An effective way to represent the holy family is to have the figures backlit behind a white curtain or screen so that their silhouettes are visible. The magi join them and remain in tableau until the hymn before the sermon is sung. The magi may return later in the service, without fanfare, bringing the bread and cup if Communion is served.

One image that unites December 25 and January 6 is the coming of the light that cannot be extinguished. The procession, therefore, is led by lighted candles, or a single candle, large enough to make an impressive entrance. Each of the magi can be preceded in the procession by a page carrying a lantern, and the lighting in the worship space should increase as they approach their destination.

Epiphany celebrations have strong associations with the sacraments. Epiphany was a special day for baptisms in early liturgies because of its connection to the revelation of God at Jesus' baptism. Water, then, is a central symbol and should be visible. One effective but rather elaborate idea is to use an electric garden fountain of running water where the "travelers" can pause to drink and wash their hands as they make their way to Bethlehem. A clear bowl of water on a table near the entrance is also effective.

Epiphany celebrated in a congregational setting is usually a Eucharistic service because of the association of Epiphany with gifts and grace. The gifts of gold, frankincense, and myrrh foreshadow the gifts Jesus gives on the cross. Gold signifies royalty, thus reminding us of his identification at his death as the "King of the Jews." Frankincense is used by a priest and symbolizes Jesus' role as the high priest who sacrifices himself for our sins. Myrrh was a sweet-smelling spice used, among other ways, to anoint bodies and therefore foretells Jesus' death for our salvation. For this reason the Eucharistic gifts of bread and wine to be offered to the people are often brought to the table on this day accompanied by the magi. The order of worship below does not include the Communion liturgy for two reasons: It may be used in an ecumenical setting where sharing the Lord's Supper is not possible, and also it is designed so that it can be led entirely by lay people. If it is used in a church, however, incorporating the order for Holy Communion is strongly suggested.

Following the service offer refreshments or a light meal in a festive setting. Epiphany is a joyous feast that encourages a party. If children are present, an appearance by La Befana at the party is in order. La Befana is the Epiphany grandmother who appears in Italy on January 6 to tell stories and bring candy or other treats to the children. Other cultural and national customs can also be honored on this occasion. Latin American and Eastern European countries have especially rich Epiphany heritages.

The Epiphany of the Lord

Greeting

The Holy Spirit reveals to us God's eternal purpose in sending Jesus Christ, born to Mary, and anointed by the Spirit. Through the gift of God's grace we have become Christ's body and sharers of the promise in Christ Jesus through the gospel *(based on Ephesians 3:1-12)*. Let us praise God's holy name.

God's name be praised.

Call to Worship

Leader: Arise, shine; for your light has come,
People: **and the glory of the Lord has risen upon you.**
Leader: Nations shall come to your light
People: **and sovereigns to the brightness of your rising.**

(Isaiah 60:1, 3)

Leader: By the tender mercy of our God,
the dawn from on high will break upon us . . .
to guide our feet in the way of peace. *(Luke 1:78-79)*

Processional Hymn "We Three Kings"

(Additional music may be required if the procession is long and the "journey" acted out.)

Opening Prayer

God of stargazers and seekers,
you led the magi to the child at Bethlehem:
Now lead us to the light of Jesus,
born in a humble village, worshiped as a king.
Bring us together in love for you and for one another.
Give us words to praise you and voices to sing of your glory.
In Jesus' name. **Amen.**

Psalm 72:1-7, 10-14

(Read by two voices or groups as follows: Voice 1: verses 1-4; Voice 2: verses 5-7; Voice 1: verses 10-11; Voice 2: verses 12-14.)

Hymn (Suggestions: "Sing Praise to God Who Reigns Above," "O Worship the King")

Gospel Reading **Matthew 2:1-12**

Hymn (Suggestions: "The First Noel," "De Tierra Lejana Venimos" [From a Distant Home])

Scriptural Reflection

(A sermon, story, or reading is given here. See, for one possibility, the reading that follows on page 124.)

Silent Reflection

(An interlude of quiet music may accompany a brief time of prayer and meditation.)

The Peace

Where God's just ruler reigns, goodness flourishes and peace abounds. The magi searched for the Prince of Peace sent from God and found the Christ Child. Let us honor Jesus' reign by greeting each other with signs of peace. The peace of Christ be with you.

The Singing of the Doxology with Alleluias

Prayers of Thanksgiving and Intercession

Gracious God,
you have sent us the light of the world,
Jesus Christ, your only Son:
Help us to carry your light
wherever people live in fear,
wherever there is need.
God, in your goodness,

hear our prayer.

We give you grateful thanks for the grace of Jesus,
for the dawning of his reign of love.
You have given us good gifts in abundance:
Help us to spread your gifts to far places
and to our neighborhood,
so that all people may enjoy a full and peaceful life.
God, in your goodness,

hear our prayer.

We thank you for going with us on all our journeys.
Be with those caught in unfamiliar landscapes,
the wanderers, longing for home.
Hear the cry of mothers everywhere
whose children are hungry and sick.
Deliver those who have no helper.
Redeem us from violence; free us from oppression.
As you showed the magi Herod's treachery,
open our eyes to powers and principalities
that use death to serve their own designs.
Make us agents of your life-giving power.
God, in your goodness,

hear our prayer.

Help us to live as children of the light,
united by your love.
Teach us to praise and glorify you by our lives,
in thanksgiving for the glorious gift of Jesus Christ, your Son.
God, in your goodness,

hear our prayer. Amen.

Hymn (Suggestions: "Go, Tell It on the Mountain," "Joy to the World")

Sending Forth

God will give us courage to leave familiar ground,
and guide us as we bring to others God's gift of love.
The peace of Christ be with you.
And also with you.

The Journey to Epiphany: A Reading

In the old country the travelers had been court advisors, learned astronomers, dreamers, stargazers. They became wanderers and searchers. They set the king's retinue to murmuring, laughing behind their backs, when news of their quest became fodder for the court gossip mill. They had determined to make a journey, an ill-advised one, into unknown territory with little idea of their final destination.

They would not become lost; that was not one of their problems. They knew the night sky and could find their way home from anywhere. The real obstacle was the uncertainty, the question of where they were going and what they would find when they got there. There were other hazards, of course: the bandits on the road, the insurgents in the hills, the scarcity of decent food and water. The deserts were trackless and blazing with heat; the mountains were treacherous, wind-swept, and cold. But one of them had a fragment of a scroll, lost long ago by Hebrew exiles. At night by the campfire he read to the others from it, and in the daytime phrases came echoing back, making the journey bearable.

Every valley shall be lifted up,
and every mountain and hill be made low;
the uneven ground shall become level
and the rough places a plain.
Then the glory of the LORD shall be revealed,
and all the people shall see it together,
for the mouth of the LORD has spoken. *(Isaiah 40:4-5)*

With no one to interpret, they were sustained by the beauty of the words and spurred on by the hope of seeing God's glory revealed. A sign had come to them, an unmistakable indicator in the sky, which they read like an open book:

For a child has been born for us,
a son given to us; . . .
and he is named
Wonderful Counselor, Mighty God,
Everlasting Father, Prince of Peace. *(Isaiah 9:6)*

A child born to rule this war-torn world in endless peace, a promised reign of justice and mercy unlike anything the earth had known: such a child must be sought and worshiped; such a destination was worth the journey. The desert seemed to bloom before their eyes. Springs of living water appeared before them on their way, and they washed and drank till they were refreshed.

They arrived at Jerusalem and, scholars that they were, decided it would be prudent to consult the local court sages. That was a mistake. The travelers had proper credentials from their king, but King Herod, Caesar's insecure puppet, was suddenly overly friendly, ingratiating, when they asked the question, "Where is the child who has been born king of the Jews?"

Herod called in everyone who might know anything, and someone did know about Micah's prophecy:

And you, Bethlehem, . . .
are by no means least among the rulers of Judah,
for from you shall come a ruler
who is to shepherd my people Israel. *(Matthew 2:6)*

Herod, it was clear, was afraid they would find a true king, and not the least of his concerns was about his own heir's succession. The wise travelers listened to their dreams and understood all this. They resolved not to return this way and become Herod's informers.

Their last night in an inn was sleepless. The innkeeper and some of his guests were loudly gaming in the courtyard below. Their room was filthy and the bed full of fleas. They got up shortly after midnight, and guided by the brilliant star, went on to Bethlehem. The star stopped over the place where the child lay, and they went inside with their gifts: gold for a king who would rule in love, frankincense for a priest who leads us to God, and myrrh for his death that their encounter with Herod had seemed to foretell.

None of them questioned the surroundings, the obvious poverty of the village and the simplicity of the home. The family shone with a holiness and peace unattainable in Herod's opulent palace. The child was truly the object of their search: the one who had God's power to deliver the needy and free the oppressed, who was born to establish a reign where righteousness will flourish and peace abound. The child had come with showers of blessing, like rain that waters the earth. The travelers' weariness disappeared; they were overwhelmed with joy; they could return to their country and live in the hope of the light they had seen in the face of the child Jesus.

There is no record that they ever told anyone in their own country of their experience. Who would believe the story of an arduous journey to the middle of nowhere, of finding a king who, by all appearances, was a poor child born to an ordinary family? But their journey has become, like the star they followed, a beacon to all who search for God's way of hope and peace. No road is too demanding; no mountain is too daunting; no desert is too fearsome. They were aliens, strangers from a strange land, and yet they led the way for others to follow. The star that guided them carried a promise from God for the homecoming of all God's people:

Lift up your eyes and look around;
    they all gather together, they come to you;
your sons shall come from far away,
    and your daughters shall be carried on their nurses' arms.
Then you shall see and be radiant;
    your heart shall thrill and rejoice. . . .
Arise, shine; for your light has come. *(Isaiah 60:4-5a, 1a)*

The Twelve Days of Christmas

Stories, Prayers, and Ideas for Keeping Christmas

✧ **Christmas Day, December 25**

> Joy to the world, the Lord is come!
> Let earth receive her King;
> let every heart prepare him room,
> and heaven and nature sing. — *Isaac Watts, 1719*

Light candles and sing as many carols as you can remember.

Read Isaiah 9:6-7 and Luke 2:8-16.

Remember the story. If children are present, ask one or more of them to tell the Christmas story in their own words, using the figures of a nativity scene as props. Ask adults to share their first memories of hearing the Christmas story.

Prayer: Remember in prayer family and friends, the hungry and homeless, the sick and sorrowing, the lonely and afraid. Ask each person to give thanks for particular Christmas joys.

God of life, you sent your Son Jesus to be born of Mary: We give you thanks with great joy. Lead us to the manger with the shepherds; teach us to sing your glory with the angels; show us the path to peace on earth; help us to keep all these marvelous things in our hearts. In Jesus' name. Amen.

✧ December 26

> Ye who now would bless the poor
> shall yourselves find blessing.
> —*"Good King Wenceslas," J. M. Neale*

We've heard the English Christmas carol that celebrates King Wenceslas, a Czech saint who was martyred in the tenth century. According to legend, the good king "went out on the Feast of Stephen" and helped a poor man who was searching for firewood in the snow. We may have forgotten, however, the background of this song. December 26 is commemorated as St. Stephen's Day, a day to renew our concern for those in need and to give thanks for God's power over death. The deacon Stephen, remembered as the first Christian martyr, was long ago given this honored place in the church-year calendar, and Christians have celebrated the day after Christmas as the "Feast of Stephen" since the fourth century.

Remembering Stephen on this day helps us focus on our mission to serve the poor in Jesus' name as Stephen did. It also reminds us of Stephen's willingness to stand up for his faith in Christ, even when it meant his own death, and of the glory that God revealed to him. Jesus came to cast out our fear, even our fear of death. At Christmastime our eyes, like Stephen's, are on the risen Christ whose coming brings us life.

Read Acts 6:3-8; 7:54-60 and reflect on Stephen's mission to spread resources to all in need throughout the community. What did Stephen say at his death that reminds us of Jesus' words from the cross? What hope do you find in the account of Stephen's vision of Jesus at God's right hand?

Songs to read or sing while candles are lighted: "In the Bleak Midwinter," "Once in Royal David's City"

Acts of Faith: December 26 in England is Boxing Day, remembered for its tradition of distributing boxes filled with good things so that all may continue the Christmas feast. Fill a box to take to a food pantry or soup kitchen. Using an encyclopedia or the Internet, find out why the historical King Wenceslas was considered "good."

Prayer: Remember in prayer workers at relief agencies and volunteers in your congregation who distribute food. Pray for victims of violence and for those who have lost loved ones at Christmastime. Give thanks for Jesus' resurrection.

God of mercy, your servant Stephen was full of grace and power. Lead us in Stephen's path of faith and give us his courage that we, like Stephen, may do wonders among the people. We praise you for the birth of our Savior, your son Jesus, in whose name we pray. Amen.

✧ December 27

> Veiled in flesh the Godhead see,
> hail the incarnate Deity,
> pleased with us in flesh to dwell,
> Jesus, our Emmanuel.
> —*"Hark! the Herald Angels Sing," Charles Wesley, 1734*

December 27 is observed in many traditions as the Feast of St. John, Apostle and Evangelist. The Gospel that bears John's name tells Jesus' story in an unusual way, starting with the great, mystifying poem of the incarnation and ending with the very human story of Jesus' cooking breakfast on the beach for his disciples after the Resurrection. John asks us to see Jesus as God's own Son, present with God from the beginning, and yet obedient, willing to leave for a time his rightful place next to God and become fully human, enjoying life in the community of mortals and weeping with his friends at life's sorrows.

John calls Jesus the "Word made flesh"—the Word of God that calls all things into being—and speaks of Jesus as "pitching a tent" with us, sharing all our experiences, even death. John also reminds us that God's glory—the glory that surrounds the shepherds and angels in Luke's Gospel—never leaves Jesus, not even on the cross. Just as Jesus descended to earth to be with us, God raises Jesus up again to bring us life.

Read John 1:1-14 and John 3:11-17 and reflect on why God sent Jesus to be born as a baby. Repeat John 3:16 aloud and talk about God's love for the world. What does *Emmanuel* mean in your life?

Songs to read or sing while candles are lighted: "O Come, All Ye Faithful," "Lo, How a Rose E'er Blooming"

Acts of Faith: If there are children present, let them try out some of the images in John's Gospel. Create a "tent" out of bedsheets to play in, for example; and when it is time for prayers, talk about the ancient Hebrews, who worshiped in a tabernacle, and why God promised to "live in a tent" with us. Adults can talk about memories of their "tenting" experiences. Using a flashlight, experiment with the light and shadows in the room or outside on a winter evening. Talk about our fears and how the light of Jesus shines in all the fearsome places of our lives.

Prayer: Pray for the homeless and those who live in the "tent cities" of the world. Give thanks for all the ways God makes a home with us.

Ever present God, you sent Jesus to be your living Word among us, the light and life of all people: Help us to let our light shine so that others may know you are with us. Bring us together to live in the light of your perfect love that overcomes the shadows and casts out our fear. We give you thanks for the joy of knowing Jesus as our friend. In his name we pray. Amen.

✧ December 28

> You need not fear King Herod,
> he will bring no harm to you;
> so rest in the arms of your mother,

who sings you a la ru.
— *Hispanic folk song, trans. John Donald Robb*

The biblical Christmas story is full of joy over the birth of the Savior, but Matthew and Luke are also aware that Jesus' life and mission had opponents. Matthew includes in the story of the magi's visit the murderous intentions of King Herod and the tragedy that followed when he learned that a new king was born in Bethlehem. Thoughtful parents generally agree that some aspects of this story are not suitable for telling to young children; but for adults and older children, facing the issues raised by the account is vital. The shocking deaths of children in great numbers from disease, neglect, hunger, and violence was a reality in Jesus' time; and it is a reality in our own time, as anyone who watches the daily news knows. To ignore such a reality, even during this joyous season, ignores the urgency of Jesus' coming, then and now.

The Holy Innocents, the vulnerable young victims of Herod's tyranny and political envy, are commemorated as martyrs in the Western Christian traditions on December 28 and in the Eastern churches on December 29. Children are precious in God's sight, and their deaths are an abomination. Jesus, through his own death and resurrection, promises an end to death's rule and calls us to oppose tyrants and institutions that disregard God's rule of life, given in abundance to all God's children.

Read Matthew 2:13-15 (16-18, with parental guidance), Matthew 18:1-6, and Revelation 21:3-4 and reflect on God's sorrow over the suffering of children. Why do you think Herod's despicable act is included in the Christmas story? What connection can you make between this story and Jesus' crucifixion and resurrection?

Songs to read or sing while candles are lighted: "Jesus Loves Me," "The First Noel"

Acts of Faith: Make "Epiphany" cards or favors for children in a local hospital. Find out about your denomination's agencies that aid children in need and tell about their work to your Sunday school class or other group. Make a New Year's commitment to support work with children abroad and in your community through contributions and volunteer time.

Prayer: Remember in prayer children whose distress you have read about in the news recently. Remember by name the children in your family and circle of friends. Give thanks for the children in your congregation and community.

God of the little ones, you have promised that you will bring home with joy those who have gone out in sorrow. Remember in your mercy all children who are in trouble. Comfort parents who weep for their children. Teach us the ways of your reign of peace through the love of children, and make us glad in your promises. In Jesus' name. Amen.

✧ December 29

> Ox and ass before him bow,
>   and he is in the manger now. . . .
> He hath opened heaven's door,
>   and ye are blest for evermore.
> —*"Good Christian Friends, Rejoice," 14th-century Latin*

Animals are reminders of God's love for all creation. In the creation poem of Genesis 1, God calls forth swarms of living creatures from the waters and brings forth every kind of domestic and wild animal on the earth, and "God saw that it was good." At the time of the flood God instructed Noah to provide a secure haven for animals, as well as for Noah's family, in the ark. A dove bore an olive branch as God's message to Noah that the waters had receded and he could safely leave the ark. God's covenant of peace, whose sign is the rainbow, is meant for the earth and all its creatures.

ThroughoutScripture, animals join us in praising God. Birds of the air, fishes and whales, beasts of the earth are called to give God praise and glory, and they have a place among the first witnesses to Jesus' birth. Mary rode to Bethlehem on a donkey before Jesus was born, and Jesus chose a donkey, a lowly work animal, to ride to Jerusalem. As the donkey carried Jesus toward the gates, the road was lined with leafy branches and his followers proclaimed him king. The donkey, the dove, and the lion lying down with the lamb: All are symbols of Jesus' reign of peace. Their place in our hearts, in our crèches, and in Christmas art of all kinds is assured.

Read Isaiah 11:6-9 and Luke 2:15-20 and reflect on the significance of animals in nativity scenes. Why are animals seen as symbols of peace and the health of creation? What do you think Paul means when he talks about setting creation free from "bondage to decay" *(Romans 8:21)* as part of our story of salvation?

Acts of Faith: Collect Christmas cards that depict biblical scenes, especially ones with animals. Reflect on what we learn from the figures, both humans and animals. Create a collage or bulletin board display using the cards. Make a Christmas tree for the birds by coating evergreen branches or pine cones with peanut butter and "decorating" them with bird seed.

Songs to read or sing while candles are lighted: "What Child Is This?" "The Friendly Beasts"

Prayer: Remember in prayer people and organizations that work to protect animals. Pray for peace and the healing of the environment. Give thanks for pets and other animal friends.

God of peace, your prophet Isaiah saw in your home a place for wolves, lambs, leopards, kids, cows, and bears to live together unharmed. Teach us to care for your creation and work for a peaceful place for all your creatures to live. We pray in the name of Jesus, the Prince of Peace. Amen.

✧ December 30

In Bethlehem they found him; Joseph and Mary mild,
seated by the manger, watching the holy child.
—*"Sing We Now of Christmas," traditional French carol*

Christmas, even in the commercial sector, is focused on the family. For many among us such a focus can be painful. It is hurtful for some individuals who are alone, living without family connections. And it is hurtful for many families who agonize over how far from the ideal held up by our culture they fall. Families today face precarious situations. Some families are broken apart, stressed by economic crises, stretched to the limit as caregivers, or hemmed in by problems. No one has a perfect family, not even at Christmas. Jesus' family wasn't perfect either, but it was holy; and there is a difference. To be holy means to be set apart by God; to live in God's household; and to be known for acts of kindness, justice, and mercy in Jesus' name. All of us are called to be holy, as families and as individuals.

The holy family of Bethlehem is looked to as a model for family life; but if we become sentimental about Mary, Joseph, and the baby, we may misjudge their situation. Joseph and Mary struggled like other parents with tough problems. They were never a "conventional" family; and while Jesus was still a baby, they were forced to flee and live like refugees. Mary and Joseph are models for us in the way they listened to God and in their courage. Mary, filled with the Holy Spirit, saw in the birth of her Son the beginning of God's great plan for changing the world into a place where the lowly are lifted up and the proud are brought low, a place where love and peace abound. Joseph willingly took on God's strange requests, accepting Mary's pregnancy and then protecting her and the child by hiding them in Egypt. God's holy families and individuals take risks and do things that are considered strange by the world's standards.

Read Luke 2:39-52; Ephesians 2:17-22 and reflect on what it means to be a human family and what it means to be a member of God's household. What does it take to have the strength and courage to live a holy life?

Songs to read or sing while candles are lighted: "Silent Night," "Angels We Have Heard on High"

Acts of Faith: Write notes to family members or friends who have been part of your Christmas celebrations past or present. Ask children to draw pictures for relatives and friends. Arrange to take a child on an outing. Join or begin a group to offer help and support for families, including single mothers.

Prayer: Remember in prayer families and individuals in distress. Pray for the refugees and the homeless. Give thanks for families, for our life in God's family, and for individuals who are helpful and supportive in your life.

God of love, you promised to make us your children: Help us to love our brothers and sisters because you first loved us. Give us the courage to share your abundant gifts so that all people have homes, food, hospitals, schools, and freedom from violence. Comfort and strengthen families in any kind of trouble. Bring us all to the joy of living in your household. In the name of Jesus our brother. Amen.

✧ December 31

My chains fell off, my heart was free,
I rose, went forth, and followed thee.
—*"And Can It Be that I Should Gain," Charles Wesley, 1739*

On this night we look toward the coming year with hope for a new beginning. At Christmas we celebrate the birth of Jesus Christ who makes all things new through his death and resurrection. Christ left God's throne and became a household slave, obedient to death on the cross, to free us from sin and our fear of death *(Philippians 2:5-11)*. The image of Jesus' becoming a slave in order to set us free was especially meaningful for Paul's churches, whose membership included Jews with ancestors who had been slaves in Egypt and also persons who were slaves of the Roman Empire.

In our own time, New Year's Eve has special significance in African American churches. It was on December 31, 1862, that news spread—mostly through Watch Night services—of the signing of the Emancipation Proclamation: "That on the first day of January, in the year of our Lord one thousand eight hundred and sixty-three, all persons held as slaves within any State . . . shall be then, thenceforward, and forever free." Abraham Lincoln had finally put an official end to the abhorrent, inhuman practice that split the United States apart. For those of us who have never experienced the degradation of slavery, the depth of joy that swept through the black congregations on that night is beyond anything we have ever felt. A project was begun in the early 1900s to write down the reactions of former slaves to the announcement that they had been freed.

The following words are from a poem by a person who remembered leaving slavery behind forty years earlier:

I looked at my hands; my hands looked new.

I looked at my feet, and they did too.*

May God's newness overtake us so that we may work faithfully for God's reign of justice and peace.

(From a transcription of slave narratives made in the early 1900s, Library of Congress, reported by Vertamae Grosvenor, NPR, "All Things Considered" [February 15, 1999].)

Read Romans 8:14-17, Galatians 4:4-7 and reflect on what Paul means when he says we are God's children, "joint heirs with Christ." Read Ephesians 3:14-19 as a prayer for the new year.

Songs to read or sing while candles are lighted: "Lift Every Voice and Sing," "My Lord, What a Morning"

Acts of Faith: Ask everyone to bring a bell to ring at midnight or with the prayer below. Encourage everyone to share their hopes—both individual and communal—for the new year.

Prayer: Remember in prayer all who are held in slavery throughout the world. Pray for those who are captive to addictions and debt. Give thanks for the freedom we enjoy as God's children. Ask God for guidance as we ask forgiveness for past sins, turn away from injustice, and work to form a community of truth and reconciliation.

Leader: God of life, we give you thanks for Jesus who came as a slave to set us free. By your Spirit, make us free to bring your hope to all people.

Response: **"Proclaim liberty throughout the land."** *(Bells ring.)*

Leader: We give you thanks that you are our rock in a weary land: By your Spirit, make us free to follow you and not be afraid.

Response: "**Proclaim liberty throughout the land.**" *(Bells ring.)*

Leader: We give you thanks that you have called us your children: By your Spirit, make us free to love all our sisters and brothers.

Response: "**Proclaim liberty throughout the land.**" *(Bells ring.)*

Leader: We give you thanks that in your reign peace abounds. By your Spirit, make us free to work for your justice.

Response: "**Proclaim liberty throughout the land.**" *(Bells ring.)*

Leader: We give you thanks for making us new people in Jesus Christ. By your Spirit, make us free to live lives pleasing to you.

Response: "**Proclaim liberty throughout the land.**" Amen. *(Bells ring.)*

from Leviticus 25:10

✧ January 1

> Come, let us use the grace divine,
>   and all with one accord,
> in a perpetual covenant
>   join ourselves to Christ the Lord.
> —*Charles Wesley, 1762*

New Year's resolutions are well-intentioned but often lack the power to be effective. In the community of faith, however, covenant renewal is a time-honored and appropriate way to start the New Year. God, indeed, promises to give us through the Holy Spirit the power to keep covenant and be faithful day by day. In our covenant with God, God promises to fulfill all that Christ Jesus, the Author and Perfecter of our faith, has begun; and we promise, with the Spirit's help, to live only for God in service to Jesus Christ. Long a tradition in the Wesleyan churches, the service of covenant renewal also has Presbyterian and Baptist roots and is an authentic response to the grace of God, experienced in the gift of Jesus Christ, the light of the world. These words are from John Wesley's Covenant Service:

Christ has many services to be done;
some are easy, others are difficult. . . .
Yet Christ strengthens us and gives us
the power to do all these things.
Therefore let us make the covenant of God our own.
Let us give ourselves completely to God,
trusting in God's promises and relying on God's grace.*

(Hoyt Hickman, et al., The New Handbook of the Christian Year [Nashville: Abingdon Press, 1992], 82)

Read Jeremiah 31:31-34; Matthew 25:31-40 and reflect on God's willingness to make a new covenant with God's people. What gives us the power to keep covenant with God? What does God expect of us?

Songs to read or sing while candles are lighted: "I Want to Walk as a Child of the Light," "A Charge to Keep I Have"

Acts of Faith: Ask everyone to suggest one way of serving God that he or she will commit to doing in the new year: teaching a class at church, visiting, praying for the sick, singing, collecting food, and sending cards are examples. Let the participants cut pictures out of old magazines to represent their area of service, glue them on poster board, and sign their names as a reminder throughout the year.

Prayer: Remember in prayer the sick and the grieving, those who are lonely and those who are troubled. Pray for the work of your congregation in the new year. Give thanks for God's forgiveness that gives us the opportunity to begin anew.

God our Creator, you have loved us with an everlasting love; through Jesus Christ we have seen your glory: Grant us grace to give ourselves completely to you. Renew us in Christ's image; empower us by the Holy Spirit to keep our baptismal promise to be your disciples. Help us to lay aside all our old fears and claim with joy the future that you hold for us. In Jesus' name. Amen.

✧ January 2

And, filled with holy joy, old Simeon in his hands
takes up the promised child, the glory of all lands.
—*"Hail to the Lord Who Comes," John Ellerton (1826–93)*

When Jesus was eight days old, Mary and Joseph took him to the Temple in Jerusalem, as was the custom according to the law of Moses, bringing two turtledoves as an offering. In the Temple they were greeted by two remarkable individuals who lived by the Scriptures and waited faithfully for God's promised Messiah. Simeon, a devout and righteous man, was led by the Holy Spirit to the Temple on that day. Simeon took the baby Jesus in his arms and praised God, saying that he could die in peace now that he had seen Jesus, God's salvation, sent for all peoples. Simeon's words became a song that has been sung at evening prayers since the earliest Christian times celebrating Jesus Christ, God's glory, given to Israel, and the light that reveals God to the Gentiles. Mary and Joseph were amazed, but Simeon had hard words for them too. He knew that Jesus would be opposed, and he warned Mary that "a sword will pierce your own soul too" *(Luke 2:35)*.

The prophet Anna was in the Temple as well, but she was there all the time. She lived in God's house, fasting and praying for the redemption of her people night and day. She was eighty-four and had been a widow most of her life. Simeon seems to have been a prominent elder, a leader whose life was dedicated to God; and Anna was from among the poor and marginalized, with no apparent family protector. Together they remind us of the variety of people who expect God's coming. Anna had lived through grief, and she greeted mourners in the Temple, weeping with them. But at the sight of the child, she began to praise God and spoke about Jesus to all who would listen. We see through the eyes of Anna and Simeon the great joy of Christ's coming.

Read Luke 2:21-40; 1 Peter 2:9-10 and reflect on the responses of Anna and Simeon to Jesus' presentation. What makes us "God's people" *(1 Peter 2:10)*?

Songs to read or sing while candles are lighted: "Hark! the Herald Angels Sing"; look in your hymnal for a hymn based on the Canticle (Song) of Simeon *(Luke 2:29-32)* and read or sing it aloud.

Acts of Faith: The event of Jesus' presentation in the Temple has its own feast day, February 2. In England this day is called Candlemas, and all the candles in the church are blessed in honor of Jesus, the light of the world. Make a votive candleholder by gluing bits of colored tissue paper on the outside of a small glass or jar to give a stained glass effect. Take the candle to a friend or relative who is housebound and read with them the story of Jesus' presentation in the Temple.

Prayer: Remember in prayer families who bring children to dedicate to God. Give thanks for the coming of Jesus and for the individuals in your life who, like Simeon and Anna, helped you see God's light.

God our hope, you sent Jesus, the light of the world, to scatter the clouds of doubt and despair. Teach us to live so that all may be touched by the light of your justice and love. Comfort all who mourn and make glad the hearts of those who wait for you. We thank you for Jesus, who makes you known to us. In his name. Amen.

✧ January 3

So when the dove descended . . .
the hidden years had ended, the age of grace began.
—*"When Jesus Came to Jordan," Fred Pratt Green, 1973*

At Christmas we celebrate the coming of God in Jesus Christ. Jesus' baptism by John in the Jordan River proclaims that the promises of Advent are being fulfilled in Jesus, the Anointed One sent from God. All four Gospels tell the story of the Spirit descending like a dove as the crowds that followed John looked on. Jesus then begins his ministry, recognized as God's beloved Son. The baptism is thus part of the story of God's coming to live among us, and the Christmas season closes with its celebration. In the Western church calendar the commemoration of the Baptism of the Lord falls on the Sunday between January 7 and 13.

Reflecting on the meaning of Jesus' baptism and on our own is also part of our devotional life during Christmas. The early church baptized adult converts after extensive teaching and preparation and usually either at Easter or Epiphany. To honor this tradition, many congregations offer a service of reaffirmation of the baptismal covenant during this season so that the promises made for us or the promises we made on our own some time ago at our baptism are fresh and significant in our lives today. By the waters of baptism we are healed and made new.

Read Mark 1:1-11; Romans 6:1-11 and reflect on what the people gathered on the banks of the Jordan saw at Jesus' baptism. In Romans what does Paul say about how baptism helps us understand Jesus' death and resurrection? What does it mean to "walk in newness of life" *(Romans 6:4)*?

Songs to read or sing while candles are lighted: "We Would See Jesus," "Hail to the Lord's Anointed"

Acts of Faith: Read the baptismal service from your denomination's hymnal or book of worship. Recall what you remember or were told about your own baptism. If children who have been baptized are present, talk to them about their baptism and encourage them to ask questions. Fill a large bowl with water and ask children and adults to put their hands in it during the prayer. As "Amen" is said, all together gently shake the water off your hands.

Prayer: Remember in prayer members of your congregation who will prepare this year for baptism, membership, or confirmation. Pray for God's guidance and a new beginning in the coming year. Give thanks in remembrance of your baptism.

Faithful God, we look to you for new life. As your Spirit anointed Jesus to heal the sick, defend the needy, and proclaim release to the captives, empower us by that Spirit to walk always in your path. Give us courage in this new year to speak your words of love to others. In Jesus' name. Amen.

✧ **January 4**

> Hope of the world, . . .
> still let thy spirit unto us be given,
> to heal earth's wounds and end all bitter strife.
> —*Georgia Harkness, 1954*

We all regret the way Christmas has been co-opted by commercial interests, but we also should remember that we have a calling to make the true story of Christmas known. Jesus was sent from God because God so loved the world. Worshiping at Jesus' birth were shepherds from the rough hillsides and wealthy sages from distant lands. No one is a foreigner at the manger; no one is excluded because of economic class. This image reminds us of the astonishing group of people who gather at the Lord's table. Though the members of some individual congregations may seem to be very much alike, we know that gathered for Communion around the world are peoples from all classes and races. God wants a full table at the banquet and is willing to send messengers into the back alleys and remote regions of the world to invite everyone in.

As God's messengers we are like the shepherds who left the stable rejoicing: we have a commission to make "known what had been told [us] about this child" *(Luke 2:18)*. The shepherds were the Internet of their day. They kept watch all night and received the news before anyone else. They were the first to hear the voices of the heralds who ran throughout the land shouting tidings of momentous events from the mountaintops. The shepherds then passed the news along as they went back to farms and villages. On Christmas the heralds were God's own angels; the news was urgent and required the shepherds' immediate action. The shepherds are a model for our own mission; we are called to follow the shepherds, "glorifying and praising God"—in words and in actions—for all we have seen and heard *(Luke 2:20)*.

Read John 17:20-24; Matthew 28:16-20 and reflect on Jesus' prayer that all his followers should be one. What do you think Jesus means when he says that he gives us his glory *(John 17:22)*? How do we share that glory with the nations?

Songs to read or sing while candles are lighted: "Go, Tell It on the Mountain," "It Came upon the Midnight Clear"

Acts of Faith: Plan an international menu for tonight's meal, or serve a tray of breads from around the world, including flat breads, whole grain breads, breads made from rice or corn. Decorate the table with pictures or objects from other nations. Begin a mission project: for example, choose a country that's been in the news because of a food crisis. Gather materials and find out how you can contribute. Plan a hunger drive now for your congregation during Lent.

God of all nations, you have come near to us, and you want us to be near to each other. Show us the way to love as Jesus loved; teach us to work for the things that make for peace. Give us voices to tell the stories of your awesome deeds and hearts that are open to all your children. For the sake of Jesus. Amen.

✧ January 5

> Brightest and best of the Stars of the morning,
> Dawn on our darkness and lend us thy aid.
> —*Reginald Heber, 1811*

January 5 is the eve of the season's last celebration for many Christians around the world and is often observed with prayer vigils and joyous festivities. In earlier times Christians celebrated Christmas on January 6, the oldest feast day in the church calendar except for Easter. Though most churches now observe Christmas on December 25, January 6 is still a major celebration for churches in the Eastern Orthodox tradition. The day celebrates the Theophany, the appearance of the Triune God: Father, Son, and Holy Spirit, and focuses on the revelation of God in Jesus when the Spirit descends at his baptism.

In Latin America the coming of the magi, *los reyes magos,* is celebrated on January 6, and the festivities of Christmas continue. In Peurto Rico, for example, children leave straw and water out for the camel, horse, and elephant of the Three Kings on January 5 and are rewarded for their kindness with small gifts. The tradition of *parrandas*, spontaneous visits to friends' homes for refreshments, and conversation continues throughout the season, ending only on January 14. For those of us who have already put away the decorations, the celebrations of our sisters and brothers in other countries are a reminder that the joy of Christmas does not end. God continues to appear in our lives and bring to us the light that cannot be overcome.

Read Psalm 72:1-7, 10-14. Read responsively if you are in a group.

Read Matthew 2:1-12 and reflect on the incredible journey of the magi. Why do you think Matthew wanted to tell a story about "foreigners" coming to worship Jesus? What characteristics of a just king are listed in Psalm 72? In what ways does Jesus fit this description?

Songs to sing or read as candles are lighted: "De Tierra Lejana Venimos" ("From a Distant Home"), "Angels from the Realms of Glory"

Acts of Faith: Have an Epiphany party with family or friends. Decorate with homemade stars, candles, and Christmas lights. The party can be simple but festive, centered around a meal or dessert. Include some traditional foods, such as a King Cake, which is a cake baked with 3 almonds dispersed in the batter; the guests who receive the almonds are given paper crowns and take the roles of the magi. Close with the reading of the Psalm and Gospel suggested above, followed by prayer and singing.

Prayer: Remember in prayer all those who celebrate this night the appearance of God among us. Pray for those who must be away from home, including those in military service, students going back to college, those in prison, foreign workers, and exiles. Give thanks for the season of Christmas and its lasting joy in our lives.

God of the wanderers, you promise to be with us and keep us on all our journeys. Give us dreams of a ladder of angels, reaching up to you. Send your star to keep our lives steady and directed to

your holy will. Protect those who are far from home. Lead us by your light. In the name of Jesus, the bright and morning star. Amen.

✧ January 6

> O Morning Star, how fair and bright
> thou beamest forth in truth and light!
> O Sovereign meek and lowly!
> —*Philipp Nicolai, 1599*

At Epiphany we remember the magi and their perilous journey into unknown territory. We also remember that Joseph was warned in a dream to take Mary and the baby and flee to Egypt. In part because of these stories of leaving home, we are especially aware of the comfort and protection of our homes at this time of year.

An Epiphany custom from Eastern Europe is the practice of blessing homes on January 6. The family or a group of friends goes from room to room expressing thanks to God and asking God to bless each room and its intended use. When the family reaches a child's bedroom, for example, the leader offers a simple prayer: "Thank you God for *Ella* and for the rest *she* receives in this room. Surround *her* with your love and keep *her* safe, that *she* may wake each day with joy and thanks. Amen." After all rooms have been blessed, the group steps outside the front door and marks the lintel in chalk with the current year and the initials C † M † B—each separated by a cross—recalling the legendary names of the magi, Caspar, Melchior, and Balthasar. As we begin a new year, we are reminded of Jesus' promise to prepare a home for us with many rooms, we give thanks for God's presence with us now, and we pray for God's blessing on all our homes.

Read Isaiah 60:1-6; John 14:1-7 and reflect on the ways God is revealed to us in Jesus Christ. What insights about God's appearing do you find in Isaiah 60:1-6? What does the coming of the light have to do with the return of families and nations? How can we put Isaiah's words into action: "Arise, shine"?

Songs to sing or read as candles are lighted: "We Three Kings," "Children, Go Where I Send Thee"

Acts of Faith: Create stars from cardboard and foil to carry to all the rooms in the house. Write a prayer to go with each star for the blessing of each room. Collect food or clothing to take to a homeless shelter in your community.

Prayer: Remember the homeless, the refugees, and all who flee from terror and oppression. Give thanks for your community, your home, and the joy of being in God's house.

God of light, we praise you for the glory that has risen upon us. We thank you for the brightness of the dawn that surrounds us all our days. Make your home with us, Lord; chase away the shadows of want and fear, and bring the nations to the light of your presence. In the name of Jesus Christ, we pray. Amen.